THE HANDBOOK OF
Preserves
A Seasonal Guide to Making Your Own

THE HANDBOOK OF
Preserves
A Seasonal Guide to Making Your Own

LINDY WILDSMITH

THE CROWOOD PRESS

First published in 2022 by
The Crowood Press Ltd
Ramsbury, Marlborough
Wiltshire SN8 2HR

enquiries@crowood.com
www.crowood.com

British Library Cataloguing-in-Publication Data
A catalogue record for this book is available from the
British Library.

ISBN 978 0 7198 4163 7

Cover design by Blue Sunflower Creative

Graphic design and typesetting by Peggy & Co. Design
Printed and bound in India by Replika Press Pvt Ltd

Contents

......

Introduction

. . . .

Today when we think of preserves, we think mostly about jams, jellies, marmalades, chutneys, cordials, pickles, ketchups and other sugared treats. These much-loved comestibles are relative newcomers to the delicious panoply of preserves. It was not until the arrival of cheap sugar from the West Indies in the nineteenth century that they appeared on the family table. Prior to this, sugar was a luxury item, reserved for the highest tables in the land, as prized and as rare as the exotic spices arriving from the East.

As we look back into our distant culinary past, instead of sugar we find salt. For hundreds of years salt was as essential, expensive and just as sought after as crude oil was throughout the twentieth century. Salt was as essential to life as breathing. Salting and drying were the only ways of preserving food. Conserved foods were the mainstay of everyone's diet from peasants to kings. Salting meat, fowl and fish in times of plenty kept everyone going through the lean winter months. Without salt, whole nations would have starved and voyages of discovery would never have been made: we might even still believe the world was flat and dreams of empire may never have been achieved.

When man discovered food lasted longer when hung near a fire, strung in the wind, buried in the sand or laid in the sun to dry, it was no longer necessary to keep moving in search of food and hunter-gatherers began to settle down near lakes or rivers. They started to make cooking pots of clay in which seawater could also be evaporated to make salt, which was able to draw moisture out of flesh, so drying it and preserving it even longer. These became essential life skills and remained so for thousands of years.

With the arrival of fridges, freezers, vacuum packs and ready-made meals in the last century, there was no longer the need to preserve food. Nonetheless we still crave the unique tastes that develop in them as chemical changes occur during processing. The texture, the colour and the taste intensifies, becoming richer and developing into new flavours. Many speculate about the fifth taste, that certain something, that quality of *savouriness*, which you cannot quite put your finger on, the deliciousness, something that is not sweet, sour, bitter or salty. The Japanese call it umami and equate it scientifically to monosodium glutamate (MSG), which exists naturally in our food. Parmesan has umami, as do sun-dried tomatoes. A stock known as *dashi*, made from ingredients including dried tuna flakes or dried mushroom, is the basis of much of Japanese cooking and imparts this special quality to the food.

◀ Well-stocked shelves featuring jars of jam, jelly, marmalade, chutney, cordial, pickles, ketchup and other treats.

As water evaporates in the preserving process, whether through drying, salting or boiling and sweetening, bacteria is held at bay, prolonging the shelf life, and intensifying and changing the flavours of the foods we eat, making them irresistible, giving them the special taste that we love.

We can, of course, simply buy these things: there are more specialists than ever working across the world, using old techniques enhanced by modern technology. There are sheds, workshops and farmhouse kitchens where confits, rillettes and potted titbits are made, as they were hundreds of years ago. There are cottage industries producing jams, chutney, bottled sauces, cordials and drinks. We have a seemingly endless appetite for good old-fashioned fayre and you will find that the ones we make ourselves are undeniably superior to even the finest artisan product.

ONCE MASTERED, THE PRESERVER'S SKILL IS INVALUABLE

Preserving fruit and vegetables, fish and meat are age-old processes that have at their core something magical: turning base metals into gold, changing water into wine, arresting the march of bacteria. Well, perhaps not as magical as alchemy, but nonetheless extraordinary.

Preserving is a skill that can be dabbled in from time to time or reward total involvement. It does not have to involve a great deal of time or expensive and complex equipment. It is a lot of fun, but you do need patience. Preserving is not an exact science: knowhow plus science over love and patience makes the best preserve. You can give as much of yourself to it as you like, and the more you give the more pleasure you will derive from it. Be warned, however: it is addictive and you will find you want to keep on experimenting.

It is a common misapprehension that preserving is a good way of using up inferior ingredients. On the contrary, use only quality produce and preserve it with the best vinegar, oil, fat, wine, herbs, sugar, salt and spice. You will only get out what you put in.

The spices and herbs we use every day, such as cinnamon, cloves, ginger, white mustard seed, aniseed, juniper, garlic and chilli peppers have antiseptic qualities. Some spices such as nutmeg, mace and aniseed also help preserve the flavour of food. Herbs like dill, thyme, bay, parsley, coriander seeds and tarragon help the preserving process. They are not there simply for flavour.

There are many methods of keeping foods, but I am going to limit myself here to those that can be made and conserved in a modern domestic kitchen, cupboard or fridge: jam, jelly, marmalade, cordial, curd, chutney, ketchup, pickle, ferment, pot, confit and rillette.

Different methodologies have evolved across the world, depending on climate and available ingredients. Fermentation involves immersion in brine, salt or wild yeasts. Pickling relies on acidic liquids such as vinegar, wine and citrus juice. Potting requires fat, whether butter, lard, duck fat, goose fat or extra-virgin olive oil. Jam, jelly and cordial require sugar. Chutney and sauces require both vinegar and sugar. I will dedicate a chapter of the book to each methodology and provide a master recipe for each protagonist, which, once learned, will empower the cook to create their own innovative preserves.

In the late twentieth century preserving was thought to be old hat, almost consigned to farmers' wives, the Women's Institute (WI) and people like me, and was on the brink of disappearing from the domestic kitchen. Today top chefs all over the world use preserving techniques to bring a new edge to the food they produce, creating innovative dishes and menus. Where daring chefs tread, others follow.

Uncover the secrets and science of preserving to learn the tricks of the trade and to find joy in simple pastimes that have been enjoyed by home cooks for decades or, in some cases, hundreds of years. Share your preserves as gifts, developing your skills, or take your new-found love to heart and even create a business. Remember that oak trees out of small acorns grow.

CHAPTER 1

Honey Without Bees

· ·

Preserving, as we know it today, was only made possible because of the introduction of cheap sugar imports from the Caribbean in the nineteenth century. Before that the principal sweetener was honey. When sugar first appeared in the West in the eleventh century it was a luxury item: the fruit conserves concocted with it were so rarefied that they were served on ornate teaspoons, as a luxurious taster to herald the close of a meal.

The joy of sugar cane was first discovered thousands of years ago by the indigenous peoples of New Guinea who chewed it. Its renown and cultivation was spread slowly by sea-faring traders to South-East Asia, India and China.

In the sixth century BC, when the Persian king Darius the Great invaded India, we are told that he found 'a reed that gives honey without bees'. A thousand years later the Arab peoples who invaded Persia in AD 651 learned how to make sugar, and traders started to sell its wondrous crystals. Its reputation seeped slowly into Western awareness around the time of the Crusades. Mentions of sugar are hard to find in Chaucer but common in Shakespeare. Queen Elizabeth I's teeth were blackened by over-consumption of this exotic white gold.

Joan of Arc was said to have taken marmelo, a preserve made with quince and sugar, and possibly a forerunner of modern marmalade, before going into battle as it gave her courage. Mary Queen of Scots kept marmelo close by as a cure-all remedy. Its mystique might have been preserved, but Spanish settlers first planted sugar canes in the New World from 1506 and the rest, as they say, is history. England

The preserves cycle (clockwise from the top): crab apple jelly, bramble, apple and brandy jam, gooseberry jelly, fig and vanilla jam, apricot conserve, damson and star anise, Seville orange marmalade, strawberry and balsamic preserve, rhubarb and orange marmalade, elderberry, apple and Sambuca jelly.

founded its first American colony at Jamestown in 1607: sugar and slaves were both present in the colony by 1619.

Like tea, coffee, tobacco, chocolate and rum, sugar was found to have comforting effects, particularly in children. In this way it escaped moral censure until late in the twentieth century, when we began to worry about the impact on our increasingly sedentary lives of overeating food high in calories and low in nutrients.

Vast amounts of sugar were imported in the seventeenth and eighteenth centuries. Consumption doubled between 1690 and 1740, but at this stage it was still a luxury item.

◄ Pouring sugar into the preserving pan.

Bread and jam for tea, the latest kitchen convenience for 20th-century factory workers.

Slavery made sugar cheaper, and the cheaper it became the more central it became to our diet. When tea and coffee, both naturally bitter, became popular in the eighteenth century, sugar became their natural partner.

As time went on a new source of sugar was discovered closer to home. In 1747 the German chemist Andreas Sigismund Marggraf discovered that beet contained the same sugar as that produced from sugar cane. His apprentice Franz Karl Achard worked on selectively breeding sugar beets and by the beginning of the nineteenth century he opened the world's first sugar beet factory.

By the end of the century cheap jam (one-third fruit pulp to two-thirds sugar) began to appear on the table of every working-class household. Women who worked in factories no longer spent their precious spare hours cooking, but like every generation that followed, embraced the latest kitchen convenience, in this case bread and jam.

There is a telling scene in the 2017 Christopher Nolan film *Dunkirk* telling the story of the Dunkirk evacuation in 1940. When the exhausted troops finally reach the safety of the boats to take them back to Blighty, they are greeted with a feast of bread and jam, which they devour with joy and relish. Sweet memories of home – no Big Macs or pizza back then!

The figures illustrating this revolution are astonishing: Britain's annual per capita consumption of sugar was 4lb in 1704, 18lb in 1800 and 90lb in 1901 – a 22-fold increase to the point where Britons had the highest sugar intake in Europe. I am happy to report that this is no longer so.

After World War II most rural (and not so rural) homes had access to a vegetable plot or allotment. This was a remnant of the famous wartime endeavour to 'Dig for Victory', introduced by the Ministry of Food to help eke out and improve the meagre rations imposed in 1940. Public gardens, parks and all available green spaces had been dug up 'to grow our own'. Even Tower Green in London did not escape the vegetable gardener's spade.

What was not eaten fresh from the ground was preserved to keep the people going through the winter. Rationing remained in place until 1954. During this time mastering the modern preserver's skills was essential. The government increased the weekly sugar ration to encourage families to preserve what they had grown, and the weekly allowance would sometimes increase from 8oz (227g) to 1lb (454g) per week.

In 1939 it had appeared as though what had been a bumper harvest would go to waste. The Women's Institute (WI), a nationwide community-based organization, came to the rescue. They successfully petitioned the government and saved 450 tons of fruit from going to waste in gardens, allotments and hedgerows by preserving it.

The following year their efforts escalated under the supervision of the Ministry of Food and they were granted £1,400 to buy sugar for jam. Rationing had been introduced and sugar was tightly controlled, records had to be kept and Preservation Centres were set up in villages where fruit was harvested. The epic endeavour was largely carried out by volunteers and significantly contributed to food supplies.

As a result 1,631 tons of preserves were made in more than 5,000 centres set up in any available space, such as kitchens and sheds, across the country, since the village halls, the WI's usual domains, were occupied by other vital war work. Some 5,300 tons of fruit were preserved between 1940 and 1945.

The WI have retained their reputation for making preserves to this very day. Members are encouraged to make, show and sell their wares. Competition is as intense as in any round of 'Strictly Come Dancing', 'The X Factor' or 'The Voice'.

The situation remained much the same through the 1950s. In the decades that followed the war, women embraced all the culinary innovations as they came along. Freshly baked bread could still be bought from the local baker, but once 'the never go stale', sliced white loaf from

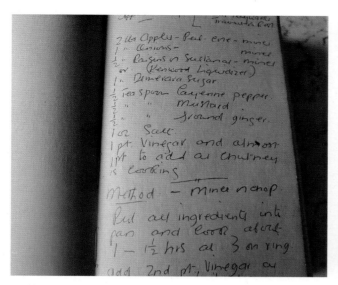

Cookbooks were handwritten collections of family recipes amassed from relations, friends and neighbours.

A kilo of fruit to a kilo of sugar makes good jam and marmalade.

Mother's Pride hit the nation, it found a permanent place in breadbins up and down the country.

The Robertson's 'golly on the jar', so beloved by generations of children, was a regular visitor to the nation's breakfast tables. How much this was due to the iconic badges that its young fans collected, or how much to fill the gaps left when money ran out for more nutritious food, I could not say, but the jars' content was sugary sweet and loved by adults and children alike, perhaps making it an early signpost to the state of the nation's waistline today.

Come the end of summer and the beginning of autumn, pantries would be stacked floor to ceiling with piles of jam jars, Kilners and bottles filled with colourful conserves. The pages of family cookbooks were filled with handwritten recipes: Mother Haywood's apple chutney, Dolly Nash's strawberry jam, Grandma's Yorkshire pudding, Dora Phillips's parsnip wine, Bren's custard creams. These neighbourly doyennes of the kitchen passed on their wealth of culinary tricks and secrets long before the advent of the TV chef.

Sugar is at the heart of preserves as we think of them today. All have common ingredients – fruit, vegetables and sugar – and in most cases the traditional ratio is a kilo of fruit to a kilo of refined sugar for jam, less for chutney. Add more sugar and the preserves become crystalline, less sugar and it will not keep for so long, unless pasteurized or kept in the fridge or freezer.

As the twentieth century rolled on, traditional kitchen crafts waned in popularity. The 1960s had brought all kinds of labour-saving devices, the contraceptive pill and convenience foods, giving women more freedom to think and to exist beyond the home and family. The Women's Liberation movement blossomed and we threw away our bras, and with them our preserving pans. Life in 1975, according to the writer Shirley Conran, was too short to stuff a mushroom and we agreed.

The pendulum has swung slowly back until today we celebrate all things artisanal. The Covid lockdowns kicked off a veritable epidemic of banana bread baking and sough dough start-ups, while preservers' cupboards are groaning under the weight of lockdown jars. However good the niche commercial equivalent, the contents of a jar of shop-bought preserves lacks that inner glow, that depth of feeling and, frankly, the flavour that comes with making your own.

What about consuming all this sugar, I hear you say? Preserves have their place in our diets with their intense flavours and jewel-like colours. Remember those exotic spoons of deliciousness served to close a meal long ago when 'sweet' was in its infancy. Preserves – when eaten by the teaspoonful on buttered toast, on bread and butter, in a jam sandwich, with meats, fish, cheeses, pies, confits and other savoury foods, in a cake or tart – enhance our eating and complement the myriad fresh ingredients we enjoy.

Variety and moderation is the key to good eating. If we ate only what we made ourselves, with the seasonal ingredients available, our diets would become healthier and more varied, our lives less sedentary, and food waste would disappear.

CHAPTER 2

Essential Stuff

. . . .

Before getting down to the details of making your own preserves, it is worth taking some time to make a note of the simple techniques and precautions that apply to nearly all the following recipes and should become second nature as you gain more experience.

TOP TWENTY HINTS: A GUIDE TO PRESERVING

- Give yourself time: do not make preserves on a day when you need to watch the clock. Time and patience are two intangible essentials.
- Read recipes carefully ahead of time to check if there is any preparation to be done in advance such as marinating, macerating, soaking, dripping, brining or slow cooking.
- Check you have all the equipment and ingredients before you start. Have waxed paper discs and labels to hand. If using upcycled jars, you will also need cellophane discs and elastic bands or lids.
- Wash new and recycled jars and lids in warm soapy water, rinse and drain or put through the dish washer.
- Always use top-quality produce: quality in, quality out!
- Use organic citrus as it is not waxed.
- Use white granulated sugar for jam; all sugars are good for chutneys and ketchups.
- Weigh all ingredients before you start.
- Prepare, wash, chop, grate, juice and so on all produce.

The preserving kitchen.

- Invert washed jars on a baking tray to heat for 20 minutes in an oven set at 125°c to sterilize. Please note that all oven temperatures noted in this book are for fan-assisted ovens.
- Boil lids for 5 minutes and leave in the hot water until required. Drain on a clean cloth.
- Give your preserves your full attention. When you are starting out, do not try to do two things at the same time. If you must answer the phone or go to the door while your preserve is cooking, switch the heat off and pull the pan off the hot ring. Otherwise it is sure to burn or boil over.
- Soften the fruit and dissolve the sugar over low heat, stirring regularly.
- Increase the heat and boil the preserve for 5–10 minutes to set. Stir from time to time, otherwise you may burn the sugar and ruin the preserve.
- Test the set for jams and jelly. Take the pan off the heat and, using a chilled teaspoon from the freezer, pick up some of the preserve and put it back on the saucer in the *fridge*. Leave for 5 minutes to cool and then tip it up. If the preserve stays on the spoon, it is ready; if it runs off, it is not. If it isn't ready, put the spoon and saucer back in the *freezer* and put the pan back on the heat and bring it back to the boil. Boil rapidly for 5 more minutes and test again (don't forget to stir from time to time). If it is still not set, repeat the process yet again. Do not forget to switch the heat off under the pan while testing.
- Once ready, rest jams and chutneys for 10 minutes before potting to help the fruit and vegetables settle and disperse evenly.

- Pour your finished preserve into a large jug before potting, as this makes potting easier. Otherwise use a jam funnel. Take care not to overfill jars and stop at the base of the neck.
- Release trapped air bubbles in the preserve in the pots by tapping the open jar on a folded cloth. Stubborn bubbles may be released by sliding the point of a clean, sharp knife or skewer down the side of the jar. This may reduce the level of the preserve and you may need to top up the jar.
- Seal the jars, wipe with a warm damp cloth and leave to cool. Label the jars when cold with the preserve name and the date made.
- When you have finished, put the preserving pan in the sink and fill with *cold* water. Put all the sticky implements in it and leave for an hour or so. The sugar will dissolve and everything will come clean without any effort. Burnt pans may need a little biological powder and have to be soaked overnight, but always soak in cold water, not hot.

PRODUCE

Having an affinity with nature, the land and the seasons is not a prerequisite for a budding preserver. Neither is having the resources to grow your own. But it could be that the presence of these qualities, written somewhere in our DNA, may be a common denominator.

Talking to enthusiasts, I discover we share the belief that our cooking and preserving should be guided by the seasons. We are inspired by the wonderful kaleidoscope of produce that turns up through the growing year, unearthing a steady flow of fodder for our tables and preserving pans. We cannot resist the call of a rhubarb patch in spring, a fruit-laden tree or a basket of fragrant summer fruit in high summer or a hedge, heavy with berries in autumn.

We reach for the preserving pan at the merest sniff of a new crop to capture its flavour and colour, and to create delicious treats to enjoy in less fruitful times of year. You may be saying to yourself right now, 'This isn't me!' But the very fact you are reading these pages could be the first step to a lifelong addiction. Homemade preserves really do taste best and provide untold culinary pleasures.

When it comes to produce, you can choose home-grown, organic, commercially grown, from the local greengrocer, farm shop or supermarket. All that matters is that it is good quality, fresh and seasonal. Nature has a happy knack of providing the nutrients, vitamins and minerals when we most need them.

When it comes to citrus and other Mediterranean and tropical fruit and veg, however, we mostly depend on imports, but they too have their seasons. For example, the Seville, the queen of marmalade oranges, is only available for a short time in winter, triggering a frenzy of marmalade making among the cognoscenti.

It is a fallacy that preserving is a good way to use up inferior or damaged produce. The best fruit for preserving is a touch underripe. Overripe fruit makes watery, tasteless jam – use them to make purees and freeze them.

One thing to remember if you grow your own, make sure you pick your fruit when the weather is fine. Wet produce will not make good preserves and will soon go mouldy.

Fragrant summer fruit in high summer.

Hedges can be heavy with fruit and berries in autumn.

THE PRESERVER'S GUIDE TO THE SEASONS

The preserver's year starts with the arrival of Seville oranges to make marmalade and draws to a close at Christmas with cranberry relish for the turkey and mincemeat for pies. A full agenda of conserving events is jammed in between, triggered by the arrival of the steady flow of fruit and vegetables as they meander in and out of season.

In reality we are no longer constrained by the seasons. What is not grown at home is imported. Summer fruits are readily available summer, autumn, winter and spring, but they are at their finest when they are grown locally, harvested when ripe and delivered to shops the same day. In the depths of winter, when our own produce is beginning to be in short supply, our preserving pans are kept busy with the import of traditional bumper crops of tangy citrus and luscious tropical fruits. Therefore, these too, play a part in our preserving year.

At the start of the growing year, the ground is ploughed and planted in readiness for a bountiful harvest to come.

Pear and apple orchards burgeon with blossom in spring.

Strawberry plants burst into flower in early summer.

Work in the kitchen-garden is never done.

Winter

Fruit
clementine
cranberry
dried fruit
grapefruit
lemon
lime
mandarin
orange
pomegranate
tangerine

Vegetables
Brussels sprout
celeriac
celery
ginger root
Jerusalem artichoke
leek
onion
parsnip
potato
red cabbage
swede
winter cabbage

Herbs
bay
horseradish
rosemary
sage
thyme

Fish and meat
crab
duck
goose
grouse
guinea fowl
hare
lobster
mallard
partridge
pheasant
smoked haddock
turkey
venison

Spring

Fruit
banana
kiwi
mango
passion fruit
pawpaw
pineapple
rhubarb

Vegetables
asparagus
broad bean
broccoli
cauliflower
cavolo nero
elderflower
green walnut
leek
lettuce
nettles
new potato
purple sprouting
radish
spring onion
turnip

Herbs
bay
elderflower
fennel
mint
rosemary
sage
thyme
wild garlic

Fish and meat
crab
crayfish
lamb
langoustine
lobster
mackerel
prawn
salmon
shrimp
smoked haddock
trout
wood pigeon

EQUIPMENT

To start you will need a large pan of sorts, weighing scales, chopping board and knife, a wooden spoon, some upcycled jars and lids and a pack of jam pot covers (wax discs, cellophane discs, labels, and elastic bands). The time to buy a few specialist items is when you get into your stride.

Preserving pan

A preserving, jam or maslin pan, is a large, thick, flat-based pan. It is specially designed for making preserves and is therefore the perfect pan for the job. Its thick base should allow for good distribution of heat. One made of stainless steel is suited to all types of hobs (including an Aga). It should hold between 8 and 12 litres (2 gallons), have metric and imperial guide markings inside and incorporate a pouring lip. Its weight, anything between 1 and 4kg, is something else to be considered when choosing.

Preserving pan, also known as a maslin pan.

Summer

Fruit

apricot
blackberry
blueberry
cherry
currants
gooseberry
greengage
loganberry
mulberry
nectarine
peach
plum
raspberry
sloe
strawberry
tayberry

Vegetables

beetroot
broad bean
broccoli
cabbage
calabrese
capsicum
carrot
cauliflower
courgette
cucumber
fennel
French bean
garlic
lettuce
onion
pea
potato

rocket
runner bean
samphire
shallot
spinach
spring onion
squash
sweetcorn
tomato
turnip

Herbs

basil
capers
edible flowers
fennel fronds
mint
nasturtium
sweet cicely
tarragon

Fish and meat

beef
crab
crayfish
lamb
langoustine
mackerel
prawn
rabbit
shrimp
trout
venison
wild salmon
wood pigeon

Autumn

Fruit

apple
crab apple
damson
fig
pear
plum
quince

Vegetables

aubergine
beetroot
broccoli
Brussels sprout
cabbage
calabrese
capsicum
carrot
cauliflower
celeriac
celery
chicory
endive
French bean
kale
leek
marrow
onion
parsnip
potato
pumpkin
radicchio

radish
rocket
spinach
squash
swede
tomato
watercress

Herbs

lavender
rosemary
sage
thyme

Fish and meat

beef
crab
crayfish
duck
goose
grouse
guinea fowl
hare
lamb
lobster
mackerel
mallard
partridge
rabbit
turkey
venison

Some questions to ask when choosing your pan

- Does it have markings on the inside?
- Does it retain heat easily?
- Does it have a pouring lip?
- Does it have a handle for lifting?

- Is the base of the pan flat and is it specially constructed for the job?
- Is there even heat distribution?
- How heavy is the pan?

The sides of the preserving pan slope gently outwards to a wider top, allowing for better evaporation of liquids, so reducing the time it takes to cook the preserves. The pan should have a well-riveted, long and loose carry handle and a small, fixed steadying handle.

Copper preserving pans are considered a luxury alternative because of their amazing heat conductivity, which allows for longer cooking times without burning. There are drawbacks, however, since copper reacts with certain acidic fruit, and you must learn how to handle this. A recent drawback is that copper is not compatible with induction hobs.

I use my mother's old aluminium pan, which I love, even though I know aluminium now gets a bad press. I also have a smaller, more modern one in stainless steel. An aluminium pan is not compatible with induction, but I have both a gas and an induction hob for this very reason. Aluminium has good conductivity and makes exceptionally good preserves.

A jelly bag and S hook can be suspended anywhere.

Free-standing jelly bag set.

Jelly bag

If you are making jelly (a clear preserve without bits; see Chapter 3), you will need to strain the cooked fruit through a jelly bag. This can simply be a conical fabric bag hung from an S hook, on a cupboard door handle or an upturned chair or stool.

Jelly bags often come complete with a table-top stand. Some of the bags and stand-sets on the market are very flimsy and not up to the job, so when buying online, please do not choose the cheapest option.

Jam thermometer

Thermometers are unreliable. The problem is not actually with the thermometer itself but with the acidity of the preserve. Setting point occurs at around 104°C, but it varies according to the acidity of the fruit. If you prefer the security of a temperature gauge, then by all means use one, but be warned you still need to learn the visual signs too (*see* Chapter 3).

Muslin

Muslin is sold in kitchen shops along with all the other paraphernalia required for preserving. Cut squares can be used for tying up herbs and spices to add to a preserve when infuser bags are not available. A colander lined with muslin is useful for straining cordials and other drinks. Muslin can also be tied over the mouth of jars and crocks for fermenting and other processes.

A colander lined with a double layer of muslin for straining cordials.

Infuser bags

You can buy tiny ready-made, disposable (paper) or reusable (cotton fabric) drawstring bags for infusing herbs and spices, and for boiling citrus pips to extract pectin. Cut a length of string to tie the bag to the pan handle.

Infusion bags for adding whole spices and dried herbs.

Jars, bottles and lids

Your local kitchen shop can supply jars and lids. There are also websites that resemble an Aladdin's cave of jars, but first ask yourself how many perfectly good jars do you regularly throw away? It takes no time at all to accumulate a decent collection of used jars that are perfect for domestic use. If you want to make a business out of making preserves, then you will need to buy jars and lids. Some pretty jars may also be worth buying if you fancy making preserves as presents, but otherwise upcycling jars is my advice and the sustainable way to go.

The stumbling block to upcycling old jars is the removal of old labels, but I have found that the colourful 'Scrubby' cleaning cloths by Kilo can wipe the most stubborn label off a jar in next to no time. It would help if other preserve and label manufacturers followed the 'Bonne Maman' brand and used water-soluble glues. When you wash a Bonne Maman preserve jar in warm soapy water or in the dishwasher the label floats off, whereas other manufacturers' labels need serious scrubbing and scraping to remove them.

Since upcycled lids tend to become damaged over time, I put a cellophane disc under the lid as this helps fill any cracks and stops bacteria entering the jar. Alternatively, replace lids or seal the jars with a damp cellophane disc secured with an elastic band. These are available in packs of jam pot cover kits.

If you are buying jars, I suggest choosing jars from 250 to 350ml for jams and jellies, 400ml for chutneys, and 500ml to 1 litre for pickles. For cordials use bottles from 250 to 750ml capacity.

Upcycled jam jars, lids, bottles, tops, Kilners and seals.

Potting funnel

It is not essential to use a potting funnel, which are available in all good kitchen shops. The hot runny preserve can be decanted into a large jug and then poured directly into the jars. When using a funnel it is easy to overfill jars, as it is difficult to see the level under the funnel.

Potting funnel.

Large heat-resistant jug

Use a 1.5-litre sized jug for potting. Pour all runny preserves into the jug from the preserving pan over the kitchen sink. This makes filling jars and bottles very much easier and quicker.

Skimmer

A skimmer is a long-handled metal utensil with a flat round 'spoon' punctuated with holes. It is essential for skimming off sugar-scum from the surface of your preserves before potting (*see* individual recipes).

Mouli-légumes

A mouli-légumes (sometimes known as a moulin légume) is unique as it sieves and purees at the same time and is indispensable for making ketchups, vegetable sauces, fruit purees and passatas. No Italian or French household is without one, but beyond these countries you are more likely to find the miniature version for preparing baby food. Make sure you buy the full-size version, with a diameter of 24cm, as a small one is not up to the job we need it for.

Jam pot cover kits

Kitchen shops sell little cellophane packets filled with waxed discs to seal the surface of the preserve, cellophane heat-sealing covers, rubber bands to seal them and labels. Some specialist shops sell individual labels and wax discs if you do not need elastic bands and cellophane circles.

Labels

Write the name of the preserve and the date made on the label. It is tempting to use large, decorated labels, but to date the glues used are not water soluble and make removing them difficult. I use the tiny white labels supplied in the jam pot cover kits or small oval labels, both of which can be stuck to the lids or jars.

General equipment

Other than the specialist items already mentioned, you may need a wooden spoon, a zester and grater, a potato peeler, a potato masher for crushing fruit as it cooks down, a citrus squeezer, a chopping board, a couple of decent sharp knives (one large, one small), a silicone spatula, colander, sieve, measuring jug and weighing scales.

A much-used skimmer.

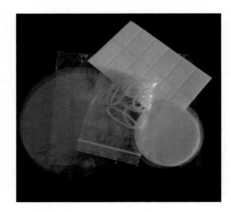

Jam pot cover kits containing wax paper discs, cellophane circles, elastic bands and labels.

Full-sized mouli-légumes for making purees and sauces.

Roll of decorative labels.

STERILIZATION

Wash all equipment thoroughly. Only jars and lids need to be sterilized.

This can be achieved simply by putting jars in the dishwasher, but it is not always convenient or environmentally sound to run a dishwasher for a few jars.

Wash the jars in warm soapy water, rinse and invert on a baking tray in a pre-heated oven set at 125°C for 20 minutes before potting. Jars must be hot ready for potting in order to contain the hot preserves without cracking.

Lids and rubber seals/gaskets should be immersed in simmering water for 5 minutes.

PASTEURIZATION OR CANNING (USA)

Pasteurization prevents certain preserves being spoiled by any remaining yeast or unwanted microbes. While methods may vary, there are three essential steps to pasteurization: heating, holding and cooling.

In the USA it is recommended that all preserves are pasteurized, but this is not required in Europe. Jam, jelly, marmalade, chutney, relishes, pickles, potted fayre and ferments are not ordinarily pasteurized as their sugar/ vinegar/salt/fat content and cooking method is sufficient to preserve the contents of the jars.

Pasteurization is recommended, however, for certain Italian preserves using olive oil as a medium.

You will need
- Large deep saucepan or boiler.
- Squat, heat-resistant glass jars, storage jars and bottles are best as they need to be immersed upright in the pasteurization pan.
- Three or four clean, thick cloths.

Method 1
- Pour the cordials or ketchups into suitably sized heat-resistant bottles or jars. Put on the caps, but do not close tightly.
- Place a thick folded cloth in the bottom of the pan.
- Put the bottles or jars in the pan upright and wind two or three clean tea towels between the jars. Add enough cold water to come just past the level of the liquid inside the bottles.
- Switch on the heat and bring the water up to the boil and simmer for 20 minutes.
- Take out the bottles, seal tightly and leave to cool on their sides to ensure the inside of the caps are sterile.

Method 2
- Put a folded cloth in the bottom of the pan. Place the jars in the middle and fill the space around them with the other folded cloths. Immerse in cold water, bring to the boil, and then simmer for 20 minutes. Leave the jars in the water until cold, then rinse and dry.
- Leave to cool and store in the dark.

When pasteurizing preserves, wrap tea towels between the jars.

Bring to the boil and simmer, using just enough water to cover the contents of the jars.

CUSTOMIZING RECIPES

Once you have mastered the basics, whether this is for jam, chutney, sauce, ferment, potted meat or fish, you will be ready to spread your wings and experiment. Each recipe comes with variations, but the table below sets out the wide range of produce you can use to make each type of preserve.

There are suggestions for which herbs and spices to use to ring the changes, and which wines and spirits to add to create truly luxurious preserves. Add spices and herbs at the start to give time for their aroma and fragrance to permeate the other ingredients. Stir in the alcohol and flowers at the end to enhance the flavours that you have created.

Ringing the changes: flavour pairing chart

Preserve	Which produce	Which herbs and spices	Which wines, spirits etc.
Marmalade	orange, blood orange, clementine, grapefruit, lemon, mandarin, pomegranate, pumpkin and citrus, quince, rhubarb and citrus, Seville orange, tangerine, apple and citrus	crushed cardamom seed, root ginger (finely grated), whole cinnamon, whole star anise	brandy, limoncello, rum, vodka, whisky
Jam, summer fruit	blackberry and apple, blackcurrant, blueberry, gooseberry, raspberry, strawberry	basil, chocolate, elderflower, lavender (brief cooking), star anise, sweet cicely, vanilla	balsamic vinegar, brandy, gin, sparkling wine, vodka
Jam, stone fruit, fig and rhubarb	apricot, blackberry, cherry, damson, dried fruit, fig, greengage, nectarine, peach, plum, rhubarb	allspice, cardamom, citrus zest, nutmeg, orange blossom water, star anise, vanilla	brandy, gin, grappa
Jam, tropical fruit spread	Mango, pawpaw, persimmon, pineapple, kiwi	black peppercorns, chilli, citrus zest and juice, tamarind	cachaça, tequila, vodka, white and dark rum
Jelly	apple, blackberry, clementine, crab apple, cranberry, elderberry, gooseberry, grape, grapefruit, hawthorn, lemon, mandarin, mulberry, orange, pomegranate, raspberry, redcurrant, rosehip, sloe, tangerine, tayberry, white currant	clove, juniper, lemon verbena, marjoram, mint, rose geranium, rosemary, sage, sweet cicely, thyme	balsamic vinegar, Cointreau, gin, Grand Marnier, vodka
Relish	cranberry, gooseberry, redcurrant, rhubarb	citrus, clove, mint, rosemary, star anise, sweet cicely, thyme	brandy, port
Curd	apricot, grapefruit, lemon, lemon and ginger, lime, orange	cardamom, ginger, Grand Marnier, salt	
Cheese/membrillo	apple, damson, pear, quince		
Cordial	berries, cinnamon, clementine, clove, elderberry, elderflower, fennel flower, ginger, ginger root, grapefruit, lemon, mandarin, orange, plum, pomegranate, rosehips, rosemary rose petals, star anise, summer fruit, sweet cicely, tangerine, thyme, vanilla		
Chutney	apple, beetroot, carrot, celeriac, courgette, date and apple, marrow, onion, pear, plum, pumpkin, rhubarb, squash, sweet potato, tomato (red and green)	allspice, bay, caraway, cardamom, cayenne, celery seed, chilli, cinnamon, clove, coriander seed, cumin seed, ginger, juniper, mustard seed, paprika, rosemary, sage, tamarind, thyme, white peppercorns	balsamic and cider vinegar, brandy, Guinness, Newcastle Brown, red and white wine vinegar, sherry vinegar, whisky

Preserve	Which produce	Which herbs and spices	Which wines, spirits etc.
Pickles	artichoke, asparagus, aubergine, baby carrot, baby cucumber (gherkins), baby courgette, beetroot, cabbage, cauliflower, cherry, crab apple, damson, dried fig, gooseberry, grape, marrow, melon, mixed veg, nasturtium seed, onion, orange, peach, pea, pear, pepper, plum, runner bean, samphire, soft walnut (July), young leek	allspice, bay, caraway, cardamom, cayenne, celery seed, chilli, cinnamon, clove, coriander seed, cumin seed, ginger, juniper, mustard seed, paprika, peppercorns, pickling spice, salt, tamarind, white peppercorns	balsamic and cider vinegar, brandy, extra-virgin olive oil, red and white wine vinegar, sherry vinegar, whisky, white wine
Sauces	apple, beetroot, mushroom, plum, tomato, elderberry	bay, basil, cayenne, celery seeds, cinnamon, cloves, garlic, green chilli, hot chilli pepper, parsley, peppercorns, pimento, salt, sweet red chilli	cider, malt, red wine, red wine and sherry vinegars, white wine, white wine and brandy
Ferments, kraut, kimchi	*Shredded*: cabbage and Chinese napa, kale and leek. *Grated*: beetroot, carrot, celeriac, daikon, fennel, ginger. *Mashed*: garlic, spinach, spring onion. *Chopped*: aubergine, cauliflower, celery, garlic, peppers. Asparagus, beetroot, carrot, cherry tomatoes, cucumber, daikon, Jerusalem artichokes, leek, peppers	allspice, berries, black mustard seed, blade mace, cardamom, cassia, celery, cinnamon, cloves, coriander, cumin, dill and caraway seeds, fennel, fenugreek, ginger, juniper berries, nigella, nutmeg, peppercorns, star anise, yellow mustard seed	
Potted	cheese, chicken, crab, ham, hare, lobster, mackerel, pheasant, rabbit, salmon, shrimp, smoked haddock, tuna, venison, guineafowl	cloves, horseradish, juniper, mace, nutmeg, parsley, peppercorns, sweet marjoram, thyme	beer, brandy, Worcester sauce
Confit	duck, pheasant, rabbit		
Rillet and rillon	pork, venison, wild boar		
Tuna	chicken, rabbit, tuna, guineafowl		

Add rose petals and other flowers to jam, jelly and chutney towards the end of the cooking time to give texture and fragrance.

Add fresh herbs to the fruit while it is cooking and then strain and drain overnight, before adding sugar and boiling it up to make jelly.

Add dried seeds and seed heads like fennel to pickles.

Put whole spices, such as cinnamon, coriander, cardamom and cumin seeds in infusion bags and boil them in the preserve.

Home-grown tomatoes make great ketchup, passata, chilli jam and chutney.

Use home-grown pears for chutney and jam. They also make great pickles for cheese.

Hedgerows can be the source of all kinds of culinary treasures. In spring they are thick with fluffy, cream elderflower blossom for cordial, which by autumn has developed into night-shaded elderberries for jelly.

From late summer onwards racemes of blackberries cascade along footpaths and country lanes. Always carry a bag in your pocket when out walking.

Bright rose hips tumble amid hedgerows and garden bushes. They are packed with vitamin C and make cordial and jelly.

Hawthorn, sloes and rowans abound. Add them for colour and flavour to hedgerow and apple jellies.

Cucamelons for pickles.

Damsons for gin.

Redcurrants for jelly.

Mini-peppers for antipasto.

Figs for jam.

Jamming: Jam, Marmalade, Jelly and Fruit Cheese

· ·

Of all preserves, homemade jam is probably the most cherished. We all have a favourite, whether strawberry, apricot, fig, cherry, greengage, damson, plum, bramble, blackcurrant or raspberry, and all others pale into insignificance.

Few, if any manufactured jams, whether mass produced or made on a small scale, come close to those made by you, your granny, uncle, mum or your friend. They simply burst with vibrancy, colour, flavour and love.

The jamming year starts straight after Christmas with the arrival of the long-awaited and sought-after bitter Seville oranges to make marmalade. What better way to spend time, after the joys of the festivities, than by making a start on preserving? The house fills with the rich fragrance of citrus and boiling sugar, bringing cheer and warmth to dreary, dark days.

JAM-BUSTING: ALL YOU NEED TO KNOW

Making jam is simple once you have some experience, but there is an ocean of useful stuff to take onboard first. My master recipes contain all the detail necessary to make delicious preserves every time, right from the word go, but you should read this first before setting out to hone your skills.

◀ A traditional afternoon tea, with jam at the centre. Jam is at the very heart of afternoon tea. Use it to fill Swiss rolls, cream slices, tarts, Victoria sponge, doughnuts, raspberry buns, Bakewell tarts and sandwiches. Alternatively, it can be spread on toast, crumpets and scones.

Three, two, one, go!

- Weigh the prepared fruit, allowing 800g–1kg of sugar for every 1kg of fruit.
- Put the fruit in a preserving pan with barely enough water to cover it.
- Simmer on low heat until the fruit collapses.
- Add the sugar, stir until dissolved, increase the heat and then boil briskly for 5 minutes.
- Test for set.
- When set, let the jam stand for 10 minutes.
- Pour, while still warm, into hot sterile jars and cover the surface with a wax disc (shiny side down) and seal with a sterile lid or dampened cellophane disc and elastic band.

Use granulated sugar, as it is cheap and makes good jam. All sugars are equal when it comes to nutritional value. There is no need to use special 'Jam Sugar', which contains pectin, unless when starting out you would welcome the extra security it brings. When adding pectin, however, you will not achieve the same depth of flavour because the jam sets quickly.

Add half a lemon when making jam, irrespective of the pectin content or the acidity of the fruit being used. Adding the juice and the lemon skin, and boiling the pips tied into a small bag or piece of muslin, helps complete the setting process. This process provides the levels of pectin and acidity necessary for the jam to set but it also balances its sweetness.

Fruit should be slightly underripe to just-ripe, rather than overripe. Pectin content is higher in underripe fruit.

There are two methods for making jam, both of which will be found in the Master Recipes below. The first, the 'overnight method' is suitable for soft fruits that need little pre-cooking. The sugar and lemon are added in advance, encouraging the fruit to make juice and the release of pectin.

The other method, known as the 'pre-cooked method', is used for stoned fruit, such as plum, apricot and peach. Cut the fruit into small pieces (there is no need to peel it), discard the stones and add enough water to just cover. Cooking the fruit pieces gently first in a little water allows it to cook and soften evenly. There is also a low sugar, tropical fruit version.

Achieving a good set is essential. Jam should be neither runny like stewed fruit nor sticky like glue. On the other hand do not expect it to set hard like jelly. A good conserve is thick with fruit pieces. To test for set, chill a plate or saucer and two teaspoons in the freezer before you start.

For a good set it is best to rely on the natural pectin and acidity in the fruit and the added lemon. The longer and slower the preserve cooks, the deeper the flavour achieved. Additives speed up the set, which can be helpful when you are starting out, but they do not enhance flavour.

It is essential to sterilize jars and lids. Do this in advance to protect preserves from lingering microbes (*see* Chapter 2).

Preserves should be potted and sealed while still hot, to help create a vacuum and protect the product from spoilage.

Soften the fruit over a gentle heat in a large heavy-based or preserving pan. Dissolve the sugar on low to medium heat, then increase the heat to high to evaporate excess moisture and thus achieve setting point.

While testing for set, switch the heat off and pull the preserving pan off the heat source, otherwise the jam will go on cooking. Overboiling can result in the jam crystallizing or the pan burning: there is no turning back from either situation. Reaching setting point can be allusive and patience is essential (*see* below).

Once you are satisfied you have a set, you should stir the jam and leave it to settle for 10 minutes. Doing this will encourage the fruit to settle evenly through the preserve in the jar, rather than floating to the top. Remember to stir the preserve once more at the end of its resting time.

White scum sometime appears on the surface of a preserve while it is boiling. Do not attempt to skim it off as it will keep on forming. Just keep stirring. If it stubbornly remains once setting point is reached, which

happens occasionally, stir in a walnut-sized knob of butter before resting.

To prevent the jars from cracking, hot preserves should be poured into hot jars. Wax discs are used to seal the top of the preserve, to protect the surface of the jam and to help keep the moisture in. If condensation forms on the inside of the jar, the wax disc forms a barrier that prevents moisture collecting on the surface of the jam.

Use recycled jars (so many are thrown away), lids, wax discs and cellophane circles. These give extra protection should microbes creep in. If you find a layer of pale green mould on the top of the wax disc, you can simply peel away the waxed paper disc.

When you have potted the last bit of preserve, put all your sticky utensils in the preserving pan in the sink and fill it up with *cold* water at least for an hour. When you come back to it, the sugar will have dissolved. No scrubbing or rubbing required! It also works for burnt pans, but soak them overnight with a little biological washing powder.

Fill the used preserving pan with cold water and the sticky residue will dissolve away.

Labels peel off when attached to warm jars, therefore wait until the preserve cools down completely before labelling.

TESTING FOR SET

Although making a preserve is a simple process, when starting out you may find that difficulties arise before you can achieve a good set. For a start, there are rules to follow and signs to recognize that come with experience.

The amount of water in the preserve affects the time it is going to take to achieve setting point. The more liquid there is to evaporate, the longer the boiling time. Buy dry, firm-looking fruit or choose a dry day when picking your own. Until you have gained some experience, test for set at 5-minute interludes.

The larger the quantity, the longer the process will take. Small quantities set quickly; I therefore recommend using between 500g and 1kg of fruit when starting out. Small quantities also work well if you like variety in your store cupboard, although large quantities are great if you have a glut of produce to use up. Traditional preserves keep for up to five years and they will not go to waste if not used within twelve months. Preserves mature with age.

How to test for set

Put two teaspoons on a small plate in the freezer before you start. When you have cooked the fruit on low heat and the added sugar has dissolved, increase the heat. Bring to the boil and boil rapidly for 10–15 minutes. Stir from time to time to check that the preserve is not catching on the bottom of the pan.

Take the pan off the heat and remove a small amount of the preserve using one of the chilled teaspoons. Put the filled spoon back on the saucer in the *fridge* (not the freezer). Leave for five minutes.

Take the saucer and spoon out of the fridge and tip up the spoon. If the preserve stays on the spoon, it is ready.

If the preserve runs off, it is not. Put the saucer and rinsed teaspoons back in the freezer.

Testing for set with a chilled spoon.

Return the pan to the heat, bring back to the boil and boil rapidly for 5 more minutes and test again (if you smell caramelization before the time is up, quickly pull the pan off the heat and test, it is ready). If it is still not set, repeat the process once more, but do not forget to switch the heat off while testing. If you overboil the preserve, the sugar will crystallize and spoil.

If the preserve is starting to set, that is slowly sliding off the spoon, boil for about 3 minutes and test again.

With some experience you will soon learn to spot the signs and not need to watch the clock so carefully. Some preserves, such as strawberry jam and marmalades, may take 15–20 minutes hard boiling to set.

Warning signs

As the preserve boils, light frothy bubbles cover the surface. The size and texture of these bubbles change as the water evaporates and the contents of the pan starts to evaporate. The bubbles become deeper and more intense across the surface and the preserve starts to look gloopy as the pectin comes into play and setting point is near.

When the preserve has boiled hard for five minutes, run the wooden spoon through it, across the middle of the bottom of the pan. If it leaves a trail and you see the metal base of the pan, it is time to test for set.

If droplets 'cling' to the wooden spoon when lifting it out of the pan, rather than simply running off in a stream, it is time to test for set.

Bubbles form on the surface as the preserve boils. After about 5 minutes run a wooden spoon across the pan. If you can see the metal base you are nearly there.

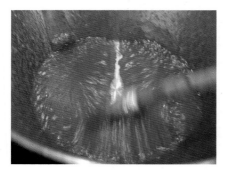

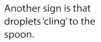
Another sign is that droplets 'cling' to the spoon.

What went wrong?

- **My preserve boiled over:** your pan was too small for the quantity of preserve being made. The pan should be deep enough to allow the fruit and juice to rise while boiling. I would recommend using an 8-litre capacity or larger preserving pan for 2kg of fruit/2kg sugar.
- **My preserve burned on the bottom of the pan:** too much prolonged heat and not enough stirring. Depending how burnt it is, it may be possible to save the pan: there's no problem if it's not too bad and has not affected the flavour, but major burning is a step too far.
- **My preserve went crystalline:** the sugar had not dissolved completely in the fruit juice when the heat was raised, and the preserve boiled. It may also have been overboiled. This is a difficult one to rectify.
- **All the fruit pieces rose to the top of the jars:** The preserve was not stirred and rested for 10 minutes before potting. Don't worry, it will still taste good and next time you will know what to do.
- **My preserve was sticky like glue:** it was overboiled. Dilute with a little boiling water and use as syrup, stirred into custard, yoghurt or lightly whipped cream.
- **My jars of preserves were runny:** it is disheartening, even annoying, if you discover your preserve is still runny when the jars have cooled down completely, but it can be rectified. Open the jars, tip the preserve back into a clean pan, note the quantity and boil it up again, adding pectin as per the manufacturer's instructions.
- **There was a layer of pale green mould on the surface of the preserve when I opened it:** it may be that microbes found their way in through a damaged lid, or that the lid had not been properly sterilized. It is also possible that the preserve was potted when lukewarm: always pot when the preserve is still piping hot. In any event, if the green mould is on the waxed paper, simply peel it off, discard and use the preserve.
- It is nothing to worry about if a small layer of white mould settles on the surface of the preserve once the jar has been opened. It may not look too nice, but it is harmless. Simply scrape it off, wipe the mouth of the jar with a damp paper towel and use the remaining preserve.
- Preserves containing reduced quantities of sugar will need to be kept in the refrigerator once opened.

The sweet scent of caramel

Do not forget to use your nose. There is a sensory sign to observe, especially when making marmalade: always switch off the heat immediately and pull the pan off the heat when you catch the merest whiff of caramelization.

THE SCIENCE OF MAKING PRESERVES

It can be helpful to understand some science, but it is not essential. Understanding the chemistry behind preserving, however, can often help you identify how to fix the problem if things go wrong. Three factors must be in perfect balance for a jam to set: pectin, sugar and acid. If jam does not set, you can be sure that one of those factors is somehow amiss.

Pectin or Pectic polysaccharide

Pectin was first isolated by French chemist Henri Braconnot in 1825. Its name is taken from the Greek word *pektikos*, meaning 'congealed' or 'curdled'. It is a kind of structural cement found in the primary cell walls of plants, particularly in the peels, seeds and cores.

Boiling the preserve releases the pectins from the fruit; with the correct amount of sugar and acidity, the long pectin chains bind to each other via intermolecular interactions, forming what scientists call a gel network, a liquid dispersed in a solid. (Pectin forms the solid that holds the liquid together.) This is known in the kitchen as the 'setting point', which happens at approximately 104°C when the correct acidity is present. The preserve is then left to cool, the gel network 'traps' the water content of the jam, leading to setting.

The pectin content of each fruit differs: acidic fruits such as apples, citrus and blackcurrants have higher levels of pectin than soft fruit, such as strawberries, raspberries and blueberries, and stone fruit such as peaches and nectarines. Slightly underripe fruit has a higher pectin content than ripe fruit. As fruit ripens, pectin is broken down by the enzyme pectinase, the fruit becomes softer as the middle membrane breaks down and cells become separated from each other.

When a preserve is made from a low pectin fruit it can be mixed with a higher pectin fruit. Alternatively lemon juice, pips and peel may be included, or commercial pectin added. Commercial pectin is obtained from apples and the peel of citrus fruits, which have a naturally high pectin content.

By binding water molecules to itself, sugar reduces the amount of water available in the jam to the point at which it is too low for microbial growth, thus helping to ensure that the jam does not grow mould. The final sugar content of jam should be between 65 and 69 per cent for this to happen.

Used in the ratio of 1kg of sugar to 1kg of fruit to make jam, sugar ensures it can be kept at ambient temperature. Preserves with a lower sugar content must be stored in the fridge to prevent them going off, or be pasteurized.

Sugar content is vital for flavour, for helping the pectin to do its job and for preserving the natural colour of the fruit.

Pectin's setting capability is aided by sugar. It draws water to itself and away from the pectin molecules, thus decreasing the ability of the pectin to remain in separate chains.

Acids

Acids are also important in helping the pectin to set. The more acidic the fruit used to make jam, the easier it is to achieve a good set. If the ph level is low it will prevent the pectin chains from being able to form the gel network – in layman's terms, prevent it setting. To avoid this, the pH of the mixture should be roughly in the range of 2.8–3.3.

Fruits contain acids. The most common is citric acid, but malic and tartaric acids are also found in certain fruits. While some acid will be present in the fruit from which the jam is made, it may not be enough to reach the desired pH and so more must be added. That is why lemon juice is added or another fruit with a higher acidic content, such as cooking apple.

Boiling

Setting point is normally reached at around 104–5°C, when the sugar content is high enough to allow the pectin branches to join. Temperature is not a reliable indicator because it varies according to the acidity and the amount of pectin in the preserve. Using a jam thermometer is therefore no guarantee of a good set.

Fruit containing high levels of pectin

Blackcurrants	Gooseberries
Citrus peel and pips	Grapes
Apples, skin and pips	Quince
Sour plums	

Fruit containing low levels of pectin

Strawberries	Peaches
Raspberries	Nectarines
Blueberries	Elderberries
Sweet plums	Cherries
Pears	Blackberries

Lemons: a special note

Just about all the recipes in this section contain a lemon. The addition of a lemon is a kind of preserving security blanket. It adds acidity and pectin, and assures a good set whatever fruit is used. Pectin is present in the skin, juice and pips. Gather up the lemon pips and place them into a small bag, which can be tied to the pan handle and dangled in the jam as it cooks.

Lemons without pips are a blessing for a gin and tonic and for cooking fish, but are not so good for jam making. It always seems to happen that when you want pips for jam making, there will be none in the lemon you slice open. To avoid finding yourself caught short, keep a tiny box of pips in your freezer and start collecting now.

The sour of lemon balances the sweet of jam, but this sweet and sour is not to everyone's taste. If this is you, use the pips but do not use the whole lemon.

Lemon pips provide an emergency supply of pectin.

Sterilization

Sterilization is an essential part of preserving as it will destroy bacteria, yeast or fungi, thus protecting the food that goes into the jars and helping it last for a year or longer.

All equipment should be washed using hot soapy water, but it is only the jars and lids that need to be sterilized. After they have been washed and rinsed, invert the clean jars onto a baking tray and place in a hot oven at 120°C for 25 minutes. Lids should be boiled in hot water for 4 or 5 minutes and left to drain on a clean cloth.

Jars and lids can also be sterilized in a dishwasher, but please don't use a full dishwasher cycle to sterilize a few jars.

Jars must be hot when potting.

Pasteurizing or canning

Pasteurization kills yeast, mould, most spoilage and pathogenic bacteria. Named after the French chemist Louis Pasteur, who developed a method to kill microbes, this is the process by which heat is applied to food and beverages to kill pathogens and extend shelf life. Typically, the heat is below the boiling point of water (100°C or 212°F).

While pasteurization kills or inactivates microorganisms, it is not a form of sterilization because bacterial spores are not destroyed. Pasteurization extends shelf life by heat inactivation of enzymes that spoil food.

Low sugar preserves, cordials and bottled fruit need to be pasteurized to prolong their shelf life. *See* page 23 for method.

Sterilizing jars is important for the longevity of any preserve.

Lids should be boiled in hot water for 5 minutes.

Each of the recipes printed in this section are blueprints that will allow you to create any flavour jam you please: refer to the 'Ringing the changes' flavour combining chart on pages 24–25. There are three basic jam recipes: one to make any soft fruit jam, one to make any stone or hard fruit jam, and one to make a reduced sugar conserve.

There are also three styles of marmalade: the boiled, fruit, rough-cut type, the fine-cut and the combination method using rhubarb, apple or pumpkin combined with citrus. All methods are suitable for all types of citruses.

Added to these are jellies and fruit cheese recipes that give the cook the freedom to use any fruit for their execution.

Finally, there are suggested variations on each theme, plus tips for customizing your preserve with herbs, flowers, spices and spirits.

Grannie's Scones with Whipped Cream and Strawberries.

Grannie's Scones with Whipped Cream and Strawberries

Best strawberry conserve for scones and clotted cream, makes 8

200g self-raising flour
1 teaspoon bicarbonate of soda
1 teaspoon cream of tartar
Pinch of salt
25g butter from the fridge
25g caster sugar
1 free-range egg
60ml sour milk or 75ml milk with 1 tablespoon lemon juice added
1 extra egg, forked for glazing

Utensils
Straight-sided scone cutter, 6cm in diameter
Alternatively use a glass

To serve
Strawberry jam
125ml clotted, whipped cream or thick bio yoghurt
200g small fresh strawberries
Icing sugar

Preheat oven to 200°C or Gas Mark 6.

Sieve the flour with the bicarbonate of soda, cream of tartar and salt into a mixing bowl. Add the butter and rub it into the flour evenly with the tips of the fingers and then mix in the sugar. Add the egg and the milk, and work the dough into a ball quickly and lightly with a knife. The dough should be soft, moist and malleable.

Transfer the dough to a floured work surface and flatten it with the hands and shape into a round about 2–3cm thick. If the dough is too moist, simply add a little extra flour. Cut out as many scones as the dough allows. Roll the trimmings into a ball, flatten it and cut out a couple more scones. Shape the remaining trimmings into one single scone. Transfer all the scones to a baking tray. Paint with beaten egg and bake for 10–15 minutes until golden. These scones may not rise as much as you expect: do not despair – they are delicious.

While still warm, split open, spread with jam, add a spoon of whipped cream and top with a strawberry. Sprinkle with a veil of icing sugar.

Always serve scones warm. Reheat for a few minutes in a hot oven before serving.

OVERNIGHT METHOD

Best strawberry conserve

Strawberry of all jams is the crowning glory of a Devon cream tea. Its rich red, fruity succulence shines through even when in Cornwall it must sit below the cream. No other jam can compare when matched with clotted cream and scones.

It is not difficult to make, but many struggle with it. Try this overnight method: it works every time.

Enhance the basic recipe by adding balsamic vinegar, a vanilla pod or a handful of nasturtium flowers.

Makes 3 or 4 × 350g jars
- Use this recipe for all seasonal summer fruits, raspberry, tayberry, blueberry, loganberry and mulberry preserves.
- Currants – red, black, and white – will need stripping from their little clusters.
- Gooseberries will need topping and tailing.
- Rhubarb sticks will need cutting into small pieces. Older, tougher rhubarb will need stringing.
- Marrow, pumpkin and squash should be peeled, deseeded and cut into small pieces.
- (For matching spices, herbs, vinegar, wine and spirits to fruits, *see* the discussion on customizing your preserves in Chapter 2.)

Ingredients
- 1kg granulated sugar
- 1 lemon, cut in half, pips removed and tied into a small bag or piece of muslin
- 1kg strawberries. Small are best; cut large ones into small pieces. Other soft fruits, such as raspberries, can be used as they are

Equipment
- Sharp knife and chopping board
- 1 preserving pan or, when starting out, a large, deep, heavy-based pan
- Large bowl
- Small square of muslin and a piece of string or a small paper or fabric infusion bag and string
- Wooden spoon, skimmer and masher
- Large jug or ladle and jam funnel
- Saucer or small plate and 2 teaspoons
- 4 × 250–350g glass jars and lids, or cellophane discs and elastic bands
- Labels and wax discs

Before you start
- Wash the jars in warm soapy water, rinse, drain and upturn on a baking tray in an oven set at 125°C for 20 minutes.
- Put the lids in a pan, add enough water to cover, bring to the boil and boil for 5 minutes.
- Chill two teaspoons in the freezer on a saucer: these are for testing for set later (*see* pages 30–31).

1. Put the fruit in a large bowl.
2. Add the sugar, squeeze the lemon juice over the fruit and add the bag of pips. Place the squeezed lemon halves in the bowl. There is no need to stir. Cover with a clean cloth and leave overnight at room temperature or for 24 hours, if time allows.
3. Transfer the contents of the bowl to the pre-serving pan.
4. Tie the bag of pips to the pan handle and mash the fruit.
5. Put the pan on low heat and stir gently until the sugar has dissolved completely and the contents of the pan is translucent.
6. Crush the fruit well with a potato masher.

Tie the bag of lemon pips to the pan handle.

7   Once the sugar has dissolved, raise the heat and bring the fruit to the boil; boil hard for 10 minutes. As the jam boils, the bubbles will get bigger and the water content will evaporate.

8   The jam thickens as setting point nears.

9   To test for set, switch the heat off and pull the pan off the hot ring. Place a little jam on the chilled spoon and put it back on the cold saucer in the fridge (not freezer) and leave for 5 minutes. When you tip the spoon, the jam should stay on. If the jam runs off the spoon it will need to be boiled again. Bring the jam back to the boil on high heat. Once it reaches the boil, boil again for 5 minutes, pull off the heat and test again.

    Some jams made with fruit containing low levels of pectin, such as strawberry, rhubarb and squashes (*see* pages 32–33) can be tricky and need patience. Sometimes it can take forever to reach setting point and you will have to test several times. Be patient. Make sure you stir the jam from time to time: if it catches and burns the bottom of the pan, the jam will spoil.

10 When you are finally satisfied you have a set, stir the jam vigorously and leave to settle for 10 minutes.

11 Untie the bag of pips, squeeze it against the side of the pan to release any remaining pectin and then discard along with the lemon halves.

12 Occasionally the white scum that appears on the jam during boiling does not disperse when stirred and settles on the surface of the jam. If this happens, add a teaspoon of butter and stir to disperse.

13 When the jam has rested, stir well. The surface should now look clear.

When set, stir the jam vigorously.

If the white scum has not cleared, stir in a knob of butter.

When rested and stirred, the surface of the jam should now be clear.

The bubbles will get bigger as the jam boils.

The jam thickens as it approaches the setting point.

14 Decant into a large, warm sterile jug. Fill the warmed jars to the base of the neck, leaving a space of 1cm at the top. If you are not using a jug, use a ladle and jam funnel to fill the jars.

15 Cover the jam surface with wax discs and seal the jars straight away with lids or dampened cellophane circles, wet side up, secured with elastic bands. Leave to cool.

Put all the sticky utensils in the pan. Fill up with cold water and leave to stand for an hour or so. Make yourself a tea or coffee or pour yourself a glass of wine and relax. When you go back to the kitchen, you will find the sticky mess has dissolved and washing up will be simple.

Label the jars when completely cold. Store in a cool, dark cupboard. Keep for at least a month before trying. It will keep for a year or more if you can resist eating it

Always leave a space of about 1cm above the jam.

Ensure all the jars are securely sealed.

Variations

Use this method and quantities to make the following preserves. Remember that you can use any soft fruit, not only the ones prescribed:

Strawberry (or any other soft fruit) and vanilla jam
- Add the seeds of half a vanilla pod with the strawberries at step 3.

Strawberry and black pepper jam
- Add 1 teaspoon cracked pepper with the strawberries at step 3.

Strawberry and balsamic jam
- Add 1 tablespoon balsamic vinegar after successfully testing for set at step 9 when stirring.

Strawberry and nasturtium flower jam
- Add 20 nasturtium flowers (stalks removed and discarded) after successfully testing for set at step 9, then stir until wilted.

Raspberry and prosecco jam
- Add 1 glass of prosecco to raspberries in the bowl at step 1.

A handful of nasturtium flowers can be added to strawberry jam.

Gooseberry and sweet cicely jam

- Add a tied bunch of sweet cicely leaves to the pan of gooseberries and sugar at step 3. Discard at step 9.

Very berry jam

- Mix three summer fruits in equal quantity rather than using a single variety, say tayberry, strawberry and blueberry.
- Add 2 tablespoons of gin at step 10 while stirring.

Rhubarb and star anise jam

- Chop the rhubarb into bite-sized pieces, proceed as per the recipe above, adding one star anise to the fruit and sugar at step 3. Discard at step 9.

Squash, orange and ginger jam

- Peel, deseed and chop the squash, proceed as per the recipe above, adding the juice, the finely grated zest of 2 oranges and a thumbnail-sized piece of root ginger (also finely grated) at step 3.

PRE-COOKED METHOD FOR STONE AND HARD FRUIT

Best apricot conserve

Apricot is another favourite, but whereas strawberry is forever England, apricot whispers France – *petite déjeuner*, patisserie, baguette, croissant, tarte …

Apricots are imported from far-flung shores in winter and the Mediterranean in summer, but you will have to keep an eye open for them as they always seem to come and go quickly. When fresh apricots are in short supply, try making jam with dried fruit. For a luxury conserve, try combining apricot and Amaretto.

Makes 3 or 4 × 350g pots

- Use this method for cherry, plum, greengage, damson, peach or nectarine jam.
- Also use for apples and pears. Figs should be cut into small pieces. There is no need to peel.
- (For matching spices, herbs, vinegar, wine and spirits to fruits, *see* the discussion on customizing your preserves on pages 24–25.)

Ingredients

- 1–1.25kg granulated sugar
- 1kg apricots, plums, nectarines, peaches, cherries or damsons
- 1 lemon

Apricot conserve ingredients.

Equipment

- Sharp knife and chopping board
- 1 preserving pan or, when starting out, a large, deep, heavy-based pan
- Large bowl
- Small square of muslin and a piece of string or a small paper or fabric infusion bag and string
- 1 mortar and pestle or sturdy bowl and rolling pin
- Wooden spoon, skimmer and masher
- Large jug or ladle and jam funnel
- Saucer or small plate and 2 teaspoons
- 4 × 250–350g glass jars and lids, or cellophane discs and elastic bands
- Labels and wax discs

Before you start

- Wash the jars in warm soapy water, rinse, drain and upturn on a baking tray in an oven set at 125°C for 20 minutes.
- Put the lids in a pan, add enough water to cover, bring to the boil and boil for 5 minutes.
- Chill two teaspoons in the freezer on a saucer: these are for testing for set later (*see* pages 30–31).

1 Cut the apricots in half and remove the stones. Retain 6 stones and discard the rest.
2 Using a pestle and mortar or a hammer, carefully smash the stones.
3 Take out the kernels and discard any that are smashed.
4 Chop the apricot halves into bite-sized pieces.
5 Cut the lemon in half, prise out the pips and tie them into a small bag or piece of muslin.
6 Put the chopped and pitted fruit in the preserving pan with the kernels.

Add 1–2cm of water for every 1kg of fruit. The water should rest just under the level of the fruit.

Put the pan of fruit over low to medium heat and simmer until the fruit is tender. Time will vary from fruit to fruit.

Cut and stone the apricots.

Carefully smash six stones with a pestle and mortar.

Discard any smashed kernels.

Place the lemon pips in a bag or piece of muslin.

Place the fruit and kernels in the pan and add water.

7 Mash the fruit to an even pulp. A potato masher is great for this. Otherwise use the back of a wooden spoon.

8 Add the sugar and stir.

9 Add the cut lemon halves, tie the bag of pips to the pan handle and stir gently until the sugar has dissolved completely, and the contents of the pan is translucent.

   Put two teaspoons on a saucer in the freezer or fridge.

   Invert freshly washed jars on a baking tray and heat at 125°C for 20 minutes to sterilize. Never pour hot preserves into cold jars.

   Once the sugar has dissolved, raise the heat and bring the fruit to the boil.

10 Boil hard for 10 minutes. As the jam boils, the water content will evaporate, the bubbles will get bigger, and the contents of the pan will thicken. When the preserve starts to reach setting point, the wooden spoon will leave a trail on the base of the pan when you scrape it (*see* page 31).

   To test for set, switch the heat off and pull the pan off the hot ring. Place a little jam on the chilled spoon and put it back on the cold saucer in the *fridge* (not freezer) and leave for 5 minutes. When you tip the spoon, the jam should stay on. If the jam runs off the spoon it will need to be boiled again. Bring the jam back to the boil on high heat and continue to boil for 5 minutes. Then pull it off the heat and test again.

   Some jams, made with fruit containing low levels of pectin, such as strawberry, rhubarb and squashes, can be tricky and need patience. Sometimes it can take forever to reach setting point and you will have to test several times. Be patient. Make sure you stir the jam from time to time. If it catches and burns the bottom of the pan, the jam will spoil.

   When you are finally satisfied you have a set, stir the jam vigorously and leave to settle for 10 minutes.

11 Untie the bag of pips, squeeze it against the side of the pan to release any remaining pectin and then discard.

12 Stir the jam vigorously. If white scum has settled on the surface of the jam (this rarely happens), add a teaspoon of butter and stir to disperse. If the surface of the jam is clear, leave to rest for 10 minutes.

13 When the jam has rested, stir well and decant into a large, warm sterilized jug.

14 Fill the warmed jars to the base of the neck, leaving a space of 1cm at the top. If not using a jug, use a ladle and jam funnel to fill the jars.

Mash the fruit to an even pulp.

Sometimes a white scum will settle on the surface.

Add the cut lemon halves, tie on the bag of pips and stir gently.

Leave a space of about 1cm at the top of the jar.

15 Cover the jam surface with wax discs.

16 Seal the jars straight away with lids or dampened cellophane circles (wet side up), secured with elastic bands. Leave to cool.

17 Put all the sticky utensils in the pan, fill it with cold water and leave to stand for an hour or so. When you return you will find the sticky mess has dissolved and washing up will be simple.

18 Label the jars when completely cold. Store in a cool, dark cupboard and keep for at least a month before trying. It will keep for a year or more.

Variations

Use this method and quantities to make the following preserves:

Peach and cardamom

- Chop the peaches and proceed as per the above recipe. Add the crushed seeds of a teaspoon of cardamom pod with the chopped peaches at step 6.

Fig and vanilla jam

- Chop the figs, discarding the stalks, do not skin. Proceed as per the apricot recipe above. Split the vanilla pod, scrape out the seeds and add to the pan along with the pod at step 6; discard at step 10.

Damson and star anise jam

- Cut the damsons in half and proceed as per the above recipe. Add a whole star anise to the pip bag and add with the fruit and sugar at step 6 and discard at step 10.

Apricot and Amaretto jam

- Add 2 tablespoons of Amaretto at stage 12 while stirring.

Nectarine and raspberry jam

- Chop the nectarines and proceed as per the above recipe. Add 1 tablespoon of raspberry cordial at step 12 while stirring.

Pineapple and white rum jam

- At step 1, peel and chop a pineapple and add to it 1 large cooking apple, also peeled and chopped. Proceed as per the above recipe.
- Add 1 tablespoon of white rum at step 12 while stirring.

Place wax discs over the surface of the jam.

Seal the jars securely and leave to cool.

Label the jars and identify the contents clearly.

Chopped figs ready for making fig and vanilla jam.

Freshly picked damsons for making damson and star anise jam.

Reduced sugar tropical fruit conserve

Enjoy tropical fruit conserve, stirred into plain yogurt and muesli for breakfast as well as on toast.

I have never heard anyone ask for a reduced sugar cake recipe, but I am often told, 'Oh I don't eat jam', in a very holier-than-thou tone, 'it contains far too much sugar'. This is a useful recipe for anyone with health issues and for whom sugar is a no no. In this case you can use your regular sugar substitute.

A few years ago a lovely young woman came over from Mumbai with the intention of learning how to make British preserves with home produce. She brought with her a sack of Alfonso mangoes, which she shared with everyone she met between Heathrow Airport, Paddington Station and Herefordshire. These mangoes were sensational even by Alfonso standards. Quite frankly you could have mashed them and spread them on toast, they were so sweet and creamy.

We devised a very low sugar recipe that I now share with anyone who wants low sugar jam. I prefer to call it a conserve. It is delicious stirred into natural yogurt, spooned onto muesli, or spread on toast.

Because the sugar content is low, it will not keep long and must be pasteurized, which is simple enough to do but involves an extra step. Make sure the fruit you choose is good and ripe.

Use this recipe to make any tropical fruit jam. Pineapple makes for a pretty lemon-coloured jam with a very strident taste. Adding the cooking apples bulks up the tropical fruits, tones the flavour down and helps the spread thicken.

Makes 3 or 4 × 250ml pots

Ingredients
- Use one of the following: 1 very ripe pineapple, 2 mangoes, 2 pawpaw, 3 or 4 persimmons, 2 guavas, 2 papaya, or 1 melon, peeled and chopped
- 2 large cooking apples
- 1 organic lemon, juiced
- Approx. 200g granulated sugar or an appropriate amount of substitute sugar of choice

Equipment
- Sharp knife and chopping board
- 1 preserving pan or, when starting out, a large, deep, heavy-based pan
- Wooden spoon and masher
- Spoon
- 4 × 250–350g glass jars and lids, cellophane and wax discs, and elastic bands
- Labels

Before you start
- Wash the jars in warm soapy water, rinse, drain and upturn on a baking tray in an oven set at 125°C for 20 minutes.
- Put the lids in a pan, add enough water to cover, bring to the boil and boil for 5 minutes.

Papaya and apple conserve.

Papaya and apple conserve ingredients.

1   Start by preparing the fruit (in this example I made a half quantity of papaya spread).

    Peel the fruit, removing any imperfections and seeds as necessary.

    Peel, core and chop the apple.

2   Chop the fruit into bite-sized pieces.

    Weigh the chopped fruit and measure 20g of sugar for every 100g of fruit. Set aside the sugar for later use.

3   Put the fruit in the preserving pan, squeeze the lemon juice over the fruit and add 150ml of water.

4   Put the pan over low heat and cook until the fruit starts to soften, say 20–30 minutes. Break it down as it cooks with a potato masher or the back of a spoon. It may be necessary to add a little extra water if the pan dries out, but do not drown it, this is to be a thick smooth fruit spread.

    When tender, add the weighed sugar or sugar substitute and stir over low heat until it dissolves. Add more sugar to taste if the spread is not sweet enough for you.

    You are not looking for setting point: the tropical fruit preserve should be a thick pulp.

5   Stand for 10 minutes before spooning into jars.

    Cover the surface of the preserve with discs of waxed paper and seal the pots with lids or covers.

Pasteurizing

6   Before transferring the sealed jars to a large pan, fold a clean tea towel and cover the base of the pan. Alternatively use a trivet. Put the jars on the folded towel or trivet and then tuck a second clean towel around the jars to fill the space. Add enough water to come just below the lids. Bring slowly to the boil and simmer for 30 minutes. (For full details, *see* page 23.)

    Leave to cool in the water.

    Take the jars out when cold, dry, label and store in a cool dark place.

Use after a few days and within 6 months. Once open store in the fridge.

Peel and clean the papaya.

Chop the papaya and apple into bite-sized pieces.

As the fruit cooks, break it down with a potato masher.

Tropical fruit preserve should be a thick pulp.

Happiness is making marmalade!

MARMALADE: ALL YOU NEED TO KNOW

First you should decide whether to use the boiled fruit method, which makes a rough-cut citrus preserve, or the traditional method that makes a fine-cut marmalade You can make any kind of citrus marmalade, single variety or mixed using tangerines, clementines, oranges, limes, lemons, grapefruit, blood oranges as well as the classic Seville oranges. When using limes, make sure you simmer the limes until they collapse completely, as their skins are tougher than that of other citrus.

If you have an organic store near you, try making marmalade with organic fruit: organic citrus is wax free. The supermarkets are keen to sell un-waxed lemons, but fall short on un-waxed limes, oranges, Seville oranges and so on. They will be more expensive, but the extra cost is worthwhile in terms of the environment alone. (To match spices, herbs, vinegar, wine and spirits to the fruit, *see* pages 24–25.)

BOILED FRUIT METHOD

Rough-cut lemon or Seville orange and ginger marmalade

The advantages of this method are that the marmalade sets well, has a particularly zesty flavour, and appeals to those who like a rough-cut preserve. It is my 'go to' method. It takes a long time to boil the whole fruit, and then more time for the fruit to cool down before the marmalade making begins, but this can all be done in advance.

If preferred the fruit can be chopped finely in a food processor.

Rough-cut lemon and ginger marmalade ingredients.

(Left) rough-cut Seville orange marmalade, (right) fine-cut lemon marmalade.

Makes 3 or 4 × 350g pots

Ingredients
- 1kg lemons or 1kg Seville oranges or 1 grapefruit, 2 oranges and two lemons or any other citrus or mix of citrus fruit
- 1kg sugar
- 1 thumb-sized piece of root ginger
- Optional: 2 tablespoons of golden syrup or honey

Equipment
- Sharp knife and chopping board
- Preserving pan and a large sheet of silver foil or, when starting out, a large, deep, heavy-based pan
- Selection of bowls
- Wooden spoon and skimmer
- Large jug or ladle and jam funnel
- Saucer or small plate and 2 teaspoons
- 4 × 250–350g glass jars and lids, cellophane discs and elastic bands
- Labels and wax discs

Before you start
- Wash the jars in warm soapy water, rinse, drain and upturn on a baking tray in an oven set at 125°C for 20 minutes.
- Put the lids in a pan, add enough water to cover, bring to the boil and boil for 5 minutes.
- Chill two teaspoons in the freezer on a saucer; these are for testing for set later.

Cover the fruit with cold water, put the lid on the pan and bring slowly to simmering point. Cook until the fruit collapses.

Juice one lemon.

Grate the ginger.

Place the collapsed fruit on a plate.

Scrape out the pulp and pips from the lemons.

1   Scrub the fruit. Prise out any stalk ends still attached and discard.

    Put the fruit in a pan (preferably a large pan with a lid, or cover your preserving pan with a sheet of foil), and add enough cold water to cover the fruit.

2   Put the pan on low heat and cover.

3   Simmer, lid on until the fruit is tender. This will take 1–2 hours, depending on which fruit you use.

4   Juice the lemon and reserve.

5   Finely grate the ginger and reserve.

6   You will know when the fruit is ready as it collapses.

7   Put the fruit on a plate and leave until cool enough to handle.

8   Transfer the liquid from the lidded pan (if used) into the preserving pan.

9   Cut the lemons in half.

10 Scrape out the flesh and pips and add to the preserving pan containing the cooking liquid. Put this back on the heat, bring back to the boil and simmer for a good 10 minutes.

    After this time, pour through a sieve into a bowl, pressing down with the back of a wooden spoon to extract any remaining juice from the fruit pulp. Return the liquid to the preserving pan and discard the pulp and pips.

11 Start chopping the fruit rinds. It speeds up the process if you stack a few skins on top of each other.

12 Slice the rinds as thinly as possible. Alternatively, cut the fruit halves into quarters and chop them finely in a food processor.

13 Add the chopped citrus rind, the strained lemon juice and the finely grated ginger (if used) to the preserving pan and stir. Put the pan back on the heat, add the sugar and bring slowly to simmering point, stirring until it has dissolved completely, and the contents of the pan become translucent. Increase the heat, bring to the boil and boil rapidly for 10 minutes and test for set. It may well take more boiling, depending on how much water there is to boil down. Remember to stir from time to time during this time to make sure the marmalade is not sticking. When setting point is reached the whole surface of the marmalade will be covered with tiny bubbles and the contents of the pan will have thickened.

    To test for set, take the pan off the heat. Place a small amount of the marmalade on a chilled teaspoon and put it on the saucer in the *fridge* to cool. After 5 minutes, take it out of the fridge and tip up the spoon.

If the marmalade stays on the spoon, it is ready; if it runs off, it is not. (Put the saucer and teaspoons back in the *freezer*.)

Put the pan back on the heat, bring back to the boil and boil rapidly for a further 5 minutes and test again. If it is still not ready, repeat the process yet again but do not forget to switch off the heat while testing. If you overboil the preserve, the sugar will crystallize and spoil. It is advisable to test for set every 5 minutes when starting out. With experience you will soon learn to spot the signs and not need to watch the clock so carefully.

When setting point is reached, turn off the heat and stir well. If any white scum remains on the surface, stir in a teaspoon of butter to disperse it.

14 When the marmalade has rested for 10 minutes, stir well.

15 This recipe can also be used for making Seville orange marmalade. When using lemons, however, it is advisable to taste at this stage: if the marmalade is too sharp for you, add a tablespoon or so of golden syrup or honey.

Decant the marmalade into a large sterile jug. Fill the warmed jars to the base of the neck, leaving a space of 1cm at the top. If not using a jug, use a ladle and funnel to fill the jars.

16 Cover the jam surface with wax discs and seal the jars straight away with lids or dampened cellophane circles (wet side up), secured with elastic bands. Leave to cool.

Put all the sticky utensils in the pan, fill with *cold water* and leave to stand for an hour or so. When you return you will find the sticky mess has dissolved and washing up will be simple.

Label the jars when completely cold, store in a cool dark cupboard.

Keep for a month at least before trying. It should keep for a year or more.

Variations

Whisky marmalade
• Add 100ml Scotch whisky when stirring the marmalade once setting point is reached at step 13.

Slice the lemon rinds as thinly as possible.

When the marmalade has reached setting point, stir and allow it to rest.

When lids are not available, seal the jars securely with cellophane discs and elastic bands.

Oxford marmalade
• Reduce sugar by 50g. Use half and half granulated and demerara sugar, and add 50g black treacle at step 13.

Ginger marmalade
• Add 50g finely chopped stem ginger when stirring the marmalade once setting point is reached at step 13.

Dundee marmalade
• Use 4 sweet oranges and 2 lemons.

Seville orange marmalade
• Use Seville oranges instead of lemons. Make in January or February when the fruit is in season.

Red grapefruit marmalade

You can also use this method for making Seville, three fruit or any citrus marmalade: lemon, lime, grapefruit, blood orange, clementine, tangerine, easy peeler, blood orange or kumquat.

Makes 3 or 4 × 350ml jars

Ingredients

- 3 red grapefruit or 1kg citrus fruit
- 1 lemon
- 800g–1kg granulated or preserving sugar
- 1 litre water

Zest the fruit with a vegetable peeler.

Cut the zest into matchstick strips.

After the pith has been cut away, cut out each segment.

Equipment

- Sharp knife and chopping board
- 1 preserving pan or, when starting out, a large, deep, heavy-based pan
- Large bowl
- Small square of muslin or a small paper or fabric infusion bag and a piece of string
- Potato peeler or zester
- Wooden spoon, skimmer
- Large jug or ladle and jam funnel
- Saucer or small plate and 2 teaspoons
- 4 × 250–350g glass jars and lids or cellophane discs and elastic bands
- Labels and wax discs

Before you start

- To sterilize jars, wash in warm soapy water, rinse, drain and upturn on a baking tray in an oven set at 125°C for 20 minutes.
- Put the lids in a pan, add enough water to cover, bring to the boil and simmer for 5 minutes.
- Chill two teaspoons in the freezer on a saucer; these are for testing for set later.

1 Scrub the fruit, prise out any stalk ends still attached and discard.

   Zest the fruit with a vegetable peeler.

2 Pile 4 or 5 strips on top of each other and cut into matchstick strips with a sharp knife.

3 Put the finely shredded zest in a small pan with enough of the measured water to cover and simmer gently with the lid on for 20 minutes. Note that you may need to add extra water if it boils down, so keep an eye on it.

   Put the remaining measured water in the preserving pan.

4 Cut away the pith from the fruit and discard.

5 Using a chopping board and a sharp knife, cut out each segment.

   Collect the pips and reserve.

6 Put the flesh and juice into a bowl.

7 Put the segment membranes in a second bowl and reserve.

8 Cut the lemon in half, collect the pips and place them in the muslin bag.

9 Squeeze the lemon juice into the bowl containing the fruit flesh and juice. Put the lemon halves in the bowl with the segment membranes.

10 Add the membrane and lemon halves to the preserving pan containing the water. Put on medium heat, bring to the boil, and then simmer for 10 minutes. Pour this through a sieve into a bowl, pressing the contents of the sieve to extract any juice. Return the preserving liquid to the preserving pan. Discard the lemon halves and the membranes.

11 Add the sugar, pulp and juice, the zested rind and water. Tie the bag containing the pips to the pan handle. Dangle the bag into the liquid.

12 Bring slowly to simmering point, stirring until the sugar has dissolved and the contents of the pan is translucent.

   Increase the heat, bring to the boil and boil rapidly for 20 minutes and test for set. It may well take more boiling, depending how much water there is to evaporate. Remember to stir from time to time, to make sure the marmalade is not sticking.

   When setting point is reached the whole surface of the marmalade will be covered with thick glossy bubbles and the contents of the pan will have darkened and reduced.

continued overleaf

Put the flesh and juice into a bowl.

The segment membranes are put in another bowl.

Make sure the lemon juice and the halves are put in the correct bowls.

Dangle the muslin with the pips in the liquid as it simmers.

At setting point the surface is covered in glossy bubbles.

13 When testing for set, take the pan off the heat and stir.

14 Place a small amount of the marmalade on a chilled teaspoon and put it on the saucer in the fridge to cool. After 5 minutes, take it out of the fridge and tip up the spoon. If the marmalade stays on the spoon, it is ready; if it runs off, it is not. (Put the saucer and teaspoons back in the freezer.)

Then put the pan back on the heat, bring back to the boil and boil rapidly for 5 more minutes and test again. If it is still not ready repeat the process, but do not forget to switch the heat off while testing. If you overboil the preserve, the sugar will crystallize and the marmalade will spoil. It is advisable to test for set every 5 minutes when starting out. With experience you will soon learn to spot the signs.

When setting point is reached, turn off the heat and stir well.

If any white scum remains on the surface, stir in a teaspoon of butter to disperse it.

15 Untie the bag of pips, squeeze it against the side of the pan to release any remaining pectin, stir and then discard.

Stir before testing for set.

Leave a 1cm gap at the top of the jar.

16 When the marmalade has rested for 10 minutes, stir well and decant into a large sterile jug.

17 Fill the warmed jars to the base of the neck, leaving a space of 1cm at the top. If you are not using a jug, use a ladle and funnel to fill the jars.

Cover the jam surface with wax discs and seal the jars straight away with lids or dampened cellophane circles (wet side up), secured with elastic bands.

Leave to cool.

Put all the sticky utensils in the pan, fill with *cold water* and leave to stand for an hour or so. When you return you will find the sticky mess has dissolved and washing up will be simple.

Label the jars when completely cold and store in a cool, dark cupboard.

Keep for a month at least before trying. It should keep for a year or more.

Variations

Grapefruit gin marmalade
- Add 2 tablespoons of gin to the regular grapefruit marmalade recipe once setting point is reached at step 15.

Seville orange marmalade
- Instead of the grapefruit shown here, use 1kg of Seville oranges plus one lemon.

Fine-cut three fruit marmalade
- Instead of the grapefruit shown here, use 1 grapefruit, 2 sweet oranges and 2 lemons, plus one extra lemon.

Sweet lemon marmalade
- Use 1kg lemons instead of the grapefruit, omit the extra lemon and add 1–3 tablespoons of Golden Syrup or honey to taste before potting.

Lime marmalade
- Use 1kg limes instead of grapefruit, omit the extra lemon and add 1–3 tablespoons of Golden Syrup or honey to taste before potting.
- Choose half yellowish limes and half dark green, as the pale ones are juicier but the dark green ones are a great colour.
- Lime zest is much tougher than others and may need simmering for 30 minutes at step 3.

Blood orange marmalade

- Use 1kg blood oranges instead of grapefruit, plus one lemon.

Clementine fizz marmalade

- Use 1kg clementines instead of grapefruit, plus one lemon. Add 50ml prosecco once setting point is reached and stir immediately.

Kumquat and tangerine marmalade

- Use 500g of each fruit instead of the grapefruit, plus one lemon.

COMBO METHOD

Rhubarb and orange marmalade

Adding the zest and juice of citrus fruit to stewed rhubarb, apple, pear, marrow, carrot, pumpkin and other squashes creates interesting textures and flavours to light up your morning toast and butter. This recipe also makes a delicious accompaniment to potted duck and game (*see* Chapter 8) and is sumptuous poured over a steamed pudding.

If you have an allotment or vegetable patch, combo marmalade is an ideal alternative to making chutney to use up seasonal gluts of produce.

Makes 3 or 4 × 350ml jars

Ingredients

- 1kg rhubarb, butternut squash, pumpkin, marrow, carrot, apple or pear
- 800g granulated sugar
- 4 small oranges or other citrus fruit
- 2 lemons
- Cinnamon stick
- 3 cloves
- 1 teaspoon of coriander seeds

Rhubarb and orange marmalade ingredients.

Equipment

- Sharp knife and chopping board
- 1 preserving pan or, when starting out, a large, deep, heavy-based pan
- Large bowl
- 2 small squares of muslin or small paper or fabric infusion bags and a piece of string
- Potato peeler or zester
- Citrus juicer
- Potato masher
- Wooden spoon, skimmer
- Large jug or ladle and jam funnel
- Saucer or small plate and 2 teaspoons
- 4 × 250–350g glass jars and lids or cellophane discs and elastic bands
- Labels and wax discs

Before you start

- To sterilize the jars, wash in warm soapy water, rinse, drain and upturn on a baking tray in an oven set at 125°C for 20 minutes.
- Put the lids in a pan, add enough water to cover, bring to the boil and simmer for 5 minutes.
- Chill two teaspoons in the freezer on a saucer; these are for testing for set later.

Peel and dice the rhubarb.

When the rhubarb is tender, mash to a smooth paste.

Zest the oranges with a potato peeler and then cut the zest into fine matchstick strips using a sharp knife.

Juice the lemons and oranges.

Note that two muslin bags are used, one for the spices and one for the pips.

1 Peel and dice or slice the rhubarb or the vegetables chosen and put into a preserving pan. Put the cinnamon stick and the spices in a small muslin bag and tie this to the pan handle.
2 Add enough water to come just below the level of the rhubarb or vegetables. Put the pan on medium heat, bring to the boil and simmer gently until tender. Then mash to a smooth paste.
3 Zest the oranges with a potato peeler.
4 Juice the oranges and lemons, reserving the pips.
5 Add the citrus juice to the pan and stir.
6 Cut the zest into fine strips and set aside.
7 Add the sugar and stir well over low to medium heat until the sugar has dissolved.
8 Place the pips in a muslin bag and tie this to the pan handle, alongside the other bag containing the spices.
9 Add the finely sliced orange zest and stir.

    Once the sugar has dissolved, bring the pan to a fast boil for 10 minutes, then test for set.

    Switch off the heat and pull the pan off the heat. Scoop up a teaspoon of the preserve with one of the teaspoons and put it back on the saucer in the fridge. Leave for 5 minutes. If the marmalade is starting to set (that is, if the preserve stays on the spoon when you turn the spoon sideways), it is ready. If not, bring the marmalade back to the boil on high heat. When it reaches the boil, boil again for 5 minutes, pull off the heat and test again.

Add the finely sliced orange zest.

10 Make sure you keep stirring the marmalade, because if it catches on the bottom of the pan it will burn.

11 When you are finally satisfied you have a set, stir well, and then leave to stand for 10 minutes. Discard the two little muslin bags.

When the preserve has rested, stir well, and decant into a large sterile jug. Fill the warmed jars to the base of the neck, leaving a space of 1cm at the top. If not using a jug, use a ladle and funnel to fill the jars.

Cover the surface with wax discs and seal the jars with cellophane circles and lids straight away. Leave to cool then label.

Put all the dirty utensils in the saucepan, fill up with *cold water* and leave to stand for an hour or so. All the sticky mess will dissolve.

As the setting point approaches, remove the muslin bags.

Jars should always be warmed before pouring in preserves.

Variations

Butternut squash and orange marmalade
- Use butternut squash instead of rhubarb.
- Omit the cinnamon stick, cloves and coriander, and add a thumb-sized piece of finely grated root ginger to the squash. There is no need to use the bag.

Double ginger marmalade
- Use cooking apples instead of rhubarb.
- Omit the cinnamon stick, cloves and coriander, and add an egg-sized piece of ginger root instead to the muslin bag.
- Steps 3 and 4: omit the oranges.
- Step 10: add 50g of finely chopped stem ginger while stirring.

Marrow and lemon marmalade
- Use marrow instead of rhubarb.
- Steps 3 and 4: omit the oranges and instead use 4 extra lemons.

Carrot, orange and kumquat marmalade
- Use carrots instead of rhubarb.
- Steps 3 and 4: use 2 sweet oranges, 6 kumquats and 2 lemons.

Victoria sponge recipe

150g softened butter or the spread of choice
150g caster sugar
3 large eggs, beaten
150g Dove self-raising flour or gluten-free self-raising flour
2 tablespoons of warm water

Beat the butter and sugar thoroughly until light and creamy. Add the beaten egg a little at a time, beating well after each addition. Continue until all the egg has been added. Should the mixture start to curdle (separate) before all the egg has been added, fold in some of the flour. Add the remaining flour and then stir in two tablespoons of warm water.

Grease the Victoria sponge pans (approximately 7in/18cm) with a little butter, lightly flour and add half the mixture to each tin and level.

Bake for 25 minutes until golden and firm to the touch.

Leave to cool in the tin for 10 minutes, then turn out on a wire rack.

Spread the gooseberry jelly or preserve of choice on the bottom layer with a palette knife dipped in boiling water. Carefully position the second sponge on top and sprinkle with caster sugar.

Gooseberry jelly is the perfect complement to a Victoria sponge.

JELLY

Jelly is the ultimate preserve, the connoisseur's jewel in the crown. It captures the colours of nature: gooseberry green, raspberry red, blackcurrant purple, crab apple pink. When a spoon glides through jelly it leaves a cut edge as clear and bright as any gemstone.

Before your first dalliance with jelly, there are one or two things you should know. Jelly is made with the strained juice of cooked fruit. It is therefore perfect for preserving currants and other 'seedy' fruit and apples, crab apples, quince, plums, damsons and greengages, since the skin and stones are dispensed with but all the goodness is retained. These fruits are acidic and have good levels of pectin, both essentials for a good set.

Jelly is more inclined to form scum than jam, so always have to hand a teaspoon of butter to stir in before testing for set.

Once setting point is reached, work fast to pot jelly, as the whole contents of the pan sets quickly.

Jelly gives a lower yield than jam because the fruit pulp, skin and seeds are removed.

To make jelly you are going to need a jelly bag and stand, or you can improvise with an upturned chair or stool and a jelly bag (*see* page 20).

Gooseberry and elderflower jelly

Gooseberry jelly is as perfect in the middle of a Victoria sponge as it is served as an accompaniment to roast lamb or baked mackerel.

Ingredients
- 1kg gooseberries. Also use apples, quince, crab apples and pears (cut into quarters), currants (red, white and black), plums, damsons, citrus fruit. No need to chop or peel the fruit or to string the currants, or to top and tail gooseberries or to stone the plums
- A handful of elderflowers, if liked or available
- Water
- 450g granulated sugar for every 600ml of juice.
- Juice of 1 lemon

Equipment
- 3 × 350ml jars and lids
- Waxed discs, cellophane pot covers and elastic bands

Before you start

- To sterilize the jars, wash in warm soapy water, rinse, drain and upturn on a baking tray in an oven set at 125°C for 20 minutes.
- Put the lids in a pan, add enough water to cover, bring to the boil and simmer for 5 minutes.
- Chill two teaspoons in the freezer on a saucer; these are for testing for set later.

1 Wash the fruit and leave to dry in the sun or fresh air.
2 Transfer to a large pan. Add enough cold water so you see the water coming up through the fruit.

   Put the pan on medium to low heat. Cover with a tipped lid or piece of foil. Simmer the fruit until it splits open or collapses and cooks to a pulp: berries will take about 60 minutes, apples 60–90 minutes.
3 Carefully transfer the fruit to a jelly bag resting on a bowl.
4 Suspend the bag over a bowl. Leave overnight for the juices to drip. Do not be tempted to squeeze the bag as this will cause the jelly to go cloudy. After this time, measure the juice and weigh 450g of sugar to every 600ml of juice and reserve.
5 Transfer the juice to a preserving pan. If using elder-flowers, add them now and boil for 5 minutes. If not, go straight to step 7.
6 Strain and return the juice to the pan.
7 Add the sugar and the strained lemon juice. Stir. Put the pan over low heat and simmer, stirring all the while until the sugar has dissolved.

continued overleaf

Wash the gooseberries and put them in the pan. Cover with cold water and simmer until tender.

Transfer the fruit to a jelly bag.

Suspend the bag over a bowl and leave overnight.

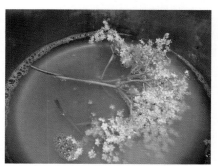

If using elderflowers, add to the juice and boil for 5 minutes.

Return the strained juice to the pan.

Increase the heat to evaporate the jelly.

As setting point approaches the bubbles become larger.

8 Increase the heat and boil rapidly. As the water evaporates, the jelly reduces.

9 The bubbles become larger until setting point is reached (5–10 minutes). After this time pull the pan off the heat.

If white scum has formed on the jelly, add a teaspoon of butter and stir well until the scum has dispersed.

10 Using one of the chilled spoons, take a half teaspoon of the jelly and put it back on the chilled saucer in the fridge. Leave for 5 minutes. After this time, if the jelly stays on the spoon when tipped it has set. If it runs off the spoon it is not ready. If so, boil again for another 5 minutes, stirring and watching that it does not stick and burn. Test again. Be patient and if necessary boil up again for another 5 minutes. The setting time depends very much on how much water is in the fruit.

11 When ready, transfer the jelly to a clean, warm, wide-mouthed jug and pour into warm sterile pots straight away. Cover the surface of the jelly with waxed paper discs (wax side down) and seal the pots with lids or covers. Leave to cool before labelling.

Store in the dark. This will keep for two years or more.

Once cooled and labelled, preserves should be transferred to a dark cupboard for storage.

Variations

Raspberry, blackcurrant and rosemary jelly

- Replace the gooseberries with 500g of raspberries, 500g of blackcurrants and a few sprigs of rosemary.

Add a few sprigs of rosemary to the raspberries and blackcurrants.

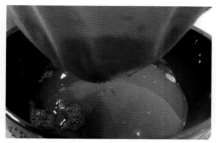

Collect the strained raspberry and blackcurrant jelly in a bowl.

Raspberry and blackcurrant jelly has a beautifully rich hue.

Redcurrant and rosemary

- If preferred you can also use loganberries, raspberries, elderberries or strawberries.
- Replace the gooseberries with 1kg of red currants and boil with a few pieces of rosemary. Continue as per the recipe for gooseberry and elderflower jelly.

After boiling for about 60 minutes the redcurrants and rosemary should be strained.

Return the redcurrant and rosemary juice to the pan before adding sugar.

Add rose petals for a luxurious finish.

Cranberry and port wine jelly

- Replace the gooseberries with 1kg cranberries. Stir two tablespoons of port into the pan at step 10 before decanting.

Crab apple jelly

- Instead of the gooseberries, boil 1.5kg crab apples, japonica fruit or quince. The delicate flavours and colours of these fruits need no additions.

Apple and sage, mint or rosemary jelly

- Replace the gooseberries with 1.5kg apples, cut in quarters and cored, Boil with a bunch of sage, mint or rosemary leaves.
- Add an extra tablespoon of finely chopped fresh sage, mint or rosemary leaves at step 10 and stir well before decanting.

Chilli and lime jelly

- Replace the gooseberries with 1.5kg cooking apples, cut in quarters and cored. Boil with 3 whole chillies.
- Cut 6–10 fresh chillies (depending on how hot you like your chilli jelly) in half lengthways. Discard the seeds and the white filaments. Chop the chilli very finely and add to the juice at step 7, together with the strained juice of a lime, and stir well before decanting.

Ensure the elderberries are dry.

Strip the berries with a fork.

Add chopped apples to the berries in the pan.

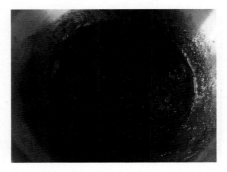
Cook until the fruit is tender, then transfer to a jelly bag and leave suspended over a bowl to drip overnight. Return the juice obtained to the pan, add the measured sugar and simmer.

Add 2 tablespoons of Sambuca before stirring and pouring into warmed jars.

Apple and elderberry jelly with Sambuca

There are certain fruits with low acidity, such as elderberry and blackberry, that are difficult to set. Adding apple can redress the balance and solve the problem.

Also use this recipe to bulk up wild berries, such as hawthorn, sloe, rosehip and rowan.

- 1kg apples
- 250g elderberries
- Juice of 1 lemon
- Sugar (weigh 200g of granulated sugar for every 300ml of juice obtained)
- 2 tablespoons of sambuca

1 Pick the elderberries on a dry day, rinse and leave to dry in the fresh air.
2 Using a fork, roughly strip the berries from the tougher stems.
3 Chop the apple: there is no need to peel. Add this to the preserving pan with the berries and enough water to come up through the fruit.
4 Cook until tender on low heat.
5 Transfer everything to a jelly bag and suspend over a bowl to drip overnight. Do not squeeze as this will cause the jelly to go cloudy.

   In the morning, measure the juice. Weigh out 200g of granulated sugar for every 300ml of juice.
6 Put the measured juice, the lemon juice and sugar in the preserving pan and put on low heat and stir until the sugar has dissolved. Then increase the heat and boil hard until setting point is reached.
7 Test for set, as described in the recipes above. Add two tablespoons of Sambuca, stir and pour into jars and seal. Label when cool.

FRUIT CHEESES

Fruit cheese is the British version of Spanish membrillo, which is made with quince and traditionally served with a cheese board at the end of a meal. Fruit cheese is made traditionally to use up the pulp left over after jelly making, but this recipe starts from scratch. Use damsons, plums, berries, apples, pears, quinces or japonica fruit.

When making fruit cheese with the pulp left over from jelly making, you should start from step 3.

Use any of the pulp left over from the jelly variations in this chapter.

I often find that by the time I have finished making jelly, I don't feel like embarking on making fruit cheese. I therefore freeze the leftover pulp to make the fruit cheese another day.

Elderberry cheese

- 1kg elderberries, gooseberries, plums, damsons, apples, pears, quince or japonica fruit
- Granulated sugar
- 1 organic lemon with pips
- Muslin bag for pips
- 1 or 2 shallow plastic boxes with lids washed in soapy water, rinsed and drained, or dishwasher washed

1 When using small fruit, such as berries and crab apples, leave them whole. Larger fruit such as quince, apples and pears should be cut into quarters. Wash and dry the fruit. Pull berries away from heavy stems.

2 Put the fruit in a preserving pan and add just a little water to cover the base. Put on low heat and bring gently to simmering point. Cook until fruit is tender and turns to a mush.

3 Transfer the fruit to a mouli-légumes and mill the fruit to separate the pulp from debris. Discard everything such as the peel and weigh the remaining fruit puree.

4 Transfer the puree to the preserving pan. Weigh an equal amount of granulated sugar and add.

5 Squeeze the lemon, strain the juice, and add to the prepared fruit with the sugar. Gather up the pips and put them in a small muslin bag. Tie the bag of pips to the pan handle.

7 Put the pan over low heat and cook until the sugar has dissolved, stirring constantly.

8 Continue cooking until the cheese thickens. This could take an hour or more, but keep stirring otherwise it will stick to the bottom of the pan and burn. Discard the pip bag.

9 When you are finally satisfied the cheese has thickened, spoon into shallow boxes, seal and cool.

10 Label and store in the refrigerator.

Put all the dirty utensils in the saucepan. Fill with *cold water* and leave to stand for an hour or so. All the sticky mess will dissolve.

Cook until the fruit turns to a mush.

A mouli-légumes separates the pulp from debris.

Measure out an equal weight of granulated sugar.

Add the sugar to the puree in the pan. Don't forget to put the lemon pips in the muslin bag.

Keep stirring as the cheese thickens.

When the cheese has thickened it can be spooned out.

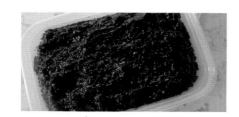
Always refrigerate any fruit cheeses.

CHAPTER 4

Sundries: Curds, Candied Peel, Christmas Mincemeat, Cranberry Relish and Cordials

• •

'Sundries' is a collection of favourite, sweet preserves that do not quite fit into the jam, marmalade or jelly category, but neither does it fit into any other. Several of the recipes are forever bound to Christmas, such as cranberry relish for the turkey and fruit mincemeat for mince pies, but not all are directly linked to the festive season, Some, like candied peel, are enjoyed throughout the year.

The first on the list, fruit curd, is not associated with the festive season, but it is difficult to categorize. Cordials could sit very nicely in a section of their own labelled 'drinks', but then there would be enough material to fill another book – and I have already covered this in *Artisan Drinks* (Jacqui Small, 2014). I have therefore included just a handful of master recipes for the most popular seasonal, fruit and flower-based cordials.

LEMON CURD AND MORE

Curd or cheese, as it is sometimes referred to (not to be confused with fruit cheese, *see* Chapter 3), is a luxurious teatime treat generally made with lemons, but orange, lime, tangerine and grapefruit curd are all worth a try. Remember to add at least one lemon when using oranges or tangerines to give that much needed zing.

Lemon curd is traditionally used to make luscious tarts, but you can use it to sandwich sponge cakes together or to fill a Swiss roll.

Stir through lightly whipped double cream, crème fraiche or mascarpone to make a richly satisfying and instant pudding, or layer with crushed meringue and raspberries for a heady, citrusy Eton Mess.

The curd we know and love today is made with eggs, sugar, the juice and zest of citrus fruit and varying amounts of butter. It is fundamentally a custard rather than the curd that its name might suggest.

The name stems originally from the eighteenth-century lemon 'curds and whey'. These were made by adding the juice of one lemon to one pint of milk, warmed in a double pan, thus forming lemon curds. The liquid was strained off to make lemon whey, which was then sweetened to taste and served warm or cold: close in name, but distant in taste and texture.

◀ Use lemon and other citrus curds to flavour possets and custards as well as in tarts.

Lemon and ginger curd ingredients.

Grate the zest and finely grate the ginger root.

Add all the other ingredients to the eggs.

Beat the mixture over a simmering pan of water.

Sieve the lemon curd.

Lemon and ginger curd

This is simply sensational as citrus curds go. Omit the ginger if you are not a fan, but treat it with caution if you are. You can use the same recipe for other flavours, but remember to add a lemon to every two oranges or tangerines for extra pizzazz.

Makes 500g

Ingredients

- 3 organic lemons
- Small egg-sized piece of root ginger
- 3 eggs
- 1 teaspoon of butter or spread
- 300g caster sugar
- 2 × clean, dry, warm, 250g jam jars or 1 × 500g jar
- Lids, cellophane and waxed paper discs, labels

Before you start

- Wash the jars in warm soapy water, rinse, drain and upturn on a baking tray in an oven set at 125°C for 20 minutes.
- Put the lids in a pan, add enough water to cover, bring to the boil and boil for 5 minutes.
- You will also need a double boiler or a heatproof bowl to sit on a suitably sized saucepan.

1 Scrub the lemons and grate the zest.
2 Peel and finely grate the ginger root.
3 Squeeze the lemon juice and strain.
4 Put the eggs in a large heatproof bowl and have the other ingredients ready.
5 Add the lemon zest, juice, grated ginger, caster sugar and butter to the eggs.
6 Sit the bowl over a pan of simmering water (make sure the simmering water does not touch the bowl) and beat the lemon and egg mixture regularly until the mixture thickens and leaves a subtle trail; this make take about 20 minutes.
7 Sieve the lemon curd.
8 The lemon curd should be smooth and creamy.

9 Transfer to a jug.

10 Pour the curd into the jar or jars.

11 Wipe the necks of the jars with a clean damp cloth, cover the surface with a waxed disc and seal the jar with a lid.

Label when cool. Store in the fridge until required.

Put all the dirty utensils in the saucepan, fill up with *cold water* and leave to stand. All the sticky mess will dissolve away.

Variations

Orange and cardamom curd

- Use 2 oranges and 1 lemon instead of 3 lemons. Add the crushed seeds of 5 cardamom pods with the other ingredients instead of the grated ginger at step 5 and sieve at step 7.

Clementine and cinnamon curd

- Use 4 clementines and 1 lemon instead of the lemons. Add a whole cinnamon stick with the other ingredients instead of the grated ginger at step 5 and discard at step 7 before straining.

Grapefruit and star anise curd

- Use 2 small grapefruit instead of the lemons, Add a whole star anise instead of the grated ginger with the other ingredients at step 5 and discard at step 7 before straining.

Lime and white rum

- Use 4 limes instead of the lemons and omit the grated ginger. Add 2 tablespoons of white rum before potting.

The lemon curd poured into the jars is smooth and creamy.

The sealed jars should be stored in the fridge.

Posset

Whisk 2 egg whites with 300ml double cream until stiff, then fold in half a jar of lemon ginger curd and spoon into custard or small wine glasses. Crush a few amaretti biscuits and sprinkle the crumbs over the possets before serving. Serve with amaretti.

Posset, made with lemon ginger curd.

MIXED CANDIED PEEL

Mixed candied peel is used a great deal in traditional winter puddings, cakes and sweetmeats, particularly at Christmas time. This is not only around our shores but also in the Mediterranean where citrus fruit grows.

Candied peel ingredients.

Make sure the rinds don't bob above the surface.

Transfer the rinds to a metal rack and dry in the oven.

The candied peel will keep for 6 weeks or more in a sterile jar.

In Sicily it is a principal ingredient of the glorious cassata: a creamy ricotta, chocolate and candied peel centre cloaked in a mantle of boozy, citrusy, sponge cake decorated with a frenzy of Baroque curlicues honed out of many-coloured candied peels and angelica.

Use citrus skins that have already been juiced if available, otherwise proceed as below.

Ingredients

- 1 lemon
- 1 orange
- ½ grapefruit
- 250g granulated sugar, plus extra for dusting
- 1 × 500g glass jar and lid

Before you start

Wash the jar in warm soapy water, rinse, drain and upturn on a baking tray in an oven set at 125°C for 20 minutes.

Put the lid in a pan, add enough water to cover, bring to the boil and boil for 5 minutes. If using a Kilner jar the lid will be attached to the jar and only the gasket (rubber seal) will need boiling.

1 Scrub the fruit and cut in half. Cut out the fruit pulp, chop and serve as a fruit salad, blitz for a smoothy or simply juice. There is no need to scrape out the pith: leaving it in will make your candied peel more succulent.

   Put the fruit rinds in a small saucepan and cover with water. Put a plate over them to weigh them down or put small weights inside the individual pieces that bob up above the surface. Bring to the boil, then reduce to a simmer and cook for 1–2 hours, or until the rinds collapse. Drain and leave to cool.

2 In the saucepan, combine the granulated sugar with 250ml of water, put on low heat and simmer until the sugar dissolves and the liquid bubbles.

   Add the rinds, stir and simmer for 25 minutes and leave to cool in the syrup overnight or until the rinds become translucent.

3 Preheat the oven to its lowest setting. Using tongs, transfer the rinds to a wire rack set over a baking tray and put in the oven for 24 hours to dry.

4 Leave to cool completely and then transfer to a sterile jar.

   Seal the jar and use as needed. It will keep for six weeks or longer.

MINCEMEAT FOR PIES

Mincemeat is not difficult to make and the homemade variety is delicious, so much richer, fresher and rounded in flavour than shop bought, which has a harsher taste altogether.

Simply chop the apples, squeeze the citrus juice, and grate the rind. Put in a bowl with the spices and sugar and stir.

Either pot in one large jar or 2 or 3 smaller ones, if that suits you better.

Ingredients

- 100g currants
- 70g sultanas
- 50g mixed peel finely diced (*see* above recipe to make your own)
- ½ teaspoon mixed spice
- ½ teaspoon grated or ground nutmeg
- Pinch ground cloves
- 250g cooking apples, pears or quince or a mixture, peeled, cored and finely chopped
- 25g blanched almonds, chopped
- 120g dark muscovado sugar
- 85g suet (vegetarians will need to buy vegetarian suet)
- Grated zest and juice of ½ lemon and ½ orange
- 2 tablespoons brandy or dark rum

- 1 × 1-litre or 3 × 350ml jars

Before you start

- Wash the jar or jars in warm soapy water, rinse, drain and upturn on a baking tray in an oven set at 125°C for 20 minutes.
- Put the lid or lids in a pan, add enough water to cover, bring to the boil and boil for 5 minutes.

1 Put all the ingredients in a large mixing bowl, stir well and cover with a clean cloth. Leave to stand overnight or for 12 hours in a cool place.
2 After this time the mixture will have darkened and be saturated by its own juice.
3 Transfer to a sterile jar or jars and seal.
4 Use straight away or store until required to make pies for Christmas.

It will keep from one year to the next if you don't use it all at Christmas.

Use Christmas mincemeat for pies and presents to share with friends and family in December.

Stir well, cover and leave overnight.

Next day the saturated mixture will be darker.

Christmas isn't the same without home-made mince pies.

Cranberry relish with orange, cinnamon and port ingredients.

Place the cinnamon and cloves in a muslin bag.

Put all the ingredients, except the port, in a pan.

When the fruit starts to pop, boil for 5 minutes.

Watch for the signs that setting point is approaching.

CRANBERRY RELISH WITH ORANGE, CINNAMON AND PORT

When it comes to turkey, cranberry relish is king. It is quick and simple to make and sets every time. Jelly is the crème de la crème for many, but the texture of the relish is more interesting, and it has tons more cranberry flavour.

Check the weight of your pack of cranberries before starting. If you have more than 250g use them all: simply add the same weight of sugar as fruit. This quantity will give enough relish for Christmas and Boxing Day for the average get-together.

As this recipe makes a small amount, there is no need to use the preserving pan. Use a medium-sized, heavy-based saucepan.

If you only have a few redcurrants, try making relish rather than jelly. The fruit goes further, but be warned the preserve will be a little seedy.

Ingredients

- 2cm cinnamon stick
- 6 whole cloves
- 250g pack fresh cranberries
- Zest and juice of 1 orange
- 250g sugar
- 1–2 tablespoons port

- 1 × 500ml or 2 × 250ml jars
- Small muslin bag
- 1 or 2 jars and lids
- Pack of jam pot covers

1 Put the cinnamon and cloves in a small muslin bag.
2 Put the cranberries in a medium-sized, heavy-based pan with the zest and juice of the orange, the bag of spices and the sugar.
3 Simmer over a low heat until the sugar dissolves and the fruit start to pop, then boil for 5 minutes until setting point is reached.

4   Take the pan off the heat and test for set. If the relish is not ready, put the pan back on the heat to boil for a few more minutes and test again.

When setting point is reached, discard the spice bag, stir in the port, skim the relish with a perforated skimmer, if necessary. Stir it well and let stand for 10 minutes for the fruit to settle. Stir and ladle into a clean, dry, warm jar or jars. Seal at once with a waxed paper disc and wipe the neck of the jar with a clean, damp cloth if necessary. Close with a lid or appropriate cover.

Let cool, label and store in a cool, dark cupboard until required. Keeps for a year or longer.

When finished, fill the pan with *cold water* to soak.

Don't forget to stir in the port when setting point has been reached.

Variation

Redcurrant and red wine relish

*   String redcurrants and proceed as above, adding the juice of a lemon but do not add spices. Add red wine instead of port to finish.

CORDIALS

Homemade cordials, like jams and jellies, have been back in vogue since the early 1980s. Elderflower and ginger are popular, but you could experiment with fruit: try blackberry, raspberry, elderberry, pomegranate (grenadine), blackcurrants, strawberry, gooseberry and plum. Or you could try elderflower or rose petals. Ring the changes by adding different herbs and spices (for further suggestions, *see* pages 24–25).

Cordials do not keep too well away from the fridge, but if you are keen to make plenty to see you through the winter, you can either freeze or pasteurize them (*see* page 23).

Pink rhubarb and elderflower cordials, diluted with sparkling water, make for a perfect alcohol-free celebration.

Put the rhubarb, star anise and lemon zest in a saucepan.

Add just half the sugar and water and make a syrup with the remaining water and sugar.

Keep stirring while bringing to the boil to dissolve the sugar.

Pour the syrup into the saucepan with the rhubarb.

Pour the mixture through a fine sieve.

Rhubarb and star anise cordial

It is not essential to use pink rhubarb, but the delicate pink hue of the resultant cordial will be your reward.

Add to cocktails, mocktails, ice cream sodas, jelly, cheesecakes and sponge cakes, as well as diluting with sparkling or still water for a ravishingly beautiful and refreshing drink.

Ingredients

- 500g young pink rhubarb
- Thinly peeled zest of 1 un-waxed lemon
- 200g granulated sugar
- 250ml cold water
- 1 star anise, root ginger or orange zest
- 1 × 500ml or 2 × 250ml bottles with screwcaps

Before you start

- Wash the bottle or bottles in warm soapy water, rinse, and drain. Put in an oven set at 125°C for 20 minutes to sterilize.
- Put the cap or caps in a pan, add enough water to cover, bring to the boil and boil for 5 minutes.

1 Rinse the rhubarb in cold running water, drain dry on a clean cloth. Cut into short lengths and put into a saucepan with the star anise and the thinly peeled lemon zest.
2 Add half the sugar and half the water.
3 Then bring gently to the boil, stirring to dissolve the sugar. Simmer for 10 minutes.
4 At the same time, put the remaining sugar in a small saucepan with the rest of the water. Gently bring to the boil, stirring to dissolve the sugar and simmer to reduce by one-third. Be careful not to reduce any further as the syrup will caramelize.
5 Pour the syrup into the saucepan of rhubarb and stir.
6 Pour the mixture through a fine sieve and leave to drain over a bowl.

Cool, then pour into a measuring jug. Check the quantity and make up to 400ml (9fl oz) with boiling water if necessary.

Fill the bottle with the spiced cordial using a funnel, leaving a small gap of 2cm between the top of the liquid and the top of the bottle. Screw down the cap firmly. Store in the fridge. If making a large quantity it should be pasteurized or frozen.

Elderflower or rose petal cordial

Garden roses make the most beautifully delicate, coloured cordials. Try experimenting with them through the summer once the elderflower has gone over. Be sure only to use unsprayed blooms. If you are lucky enough to have white jasmine in the garden, that makes a sweetly scented cordial too. *Do not use flowers that have been sprayed with chemicals.*

Makes 750ml

Ingredients

- 18 elderflower heads or 9 roses (unsprayed)
- Finely grated zest of 1 lemon
- 1 litre cold water
- 600g granulated sugar
- Juice of 1 orange and 1 lemon
- 1 teaspoon citric acid

- Muslin cloth
- 1 × 750ml or 1-litre glass bottle

Before you start

- Wash the bottle or bottles in warm soapy water, rinse and drain. Put in an oven set at 125°C for 20 minutes to sterilize.
- Put the cap or caps in a pan, add enough water to cover, bring to the boil and boil for 5 minutes.

1 Strip the flowers from the elderflower heads and put them with the finely grated lemon zest into a large deep bowl. Pour in the cold water, cover with a clean cloth, weighting the corners with clothes pegs to prevent the cloth from slipping into the liquid. Leave overnight.

2 The next day, line a colander with a double thickness of muslin and sit it on a large saucepan. Scald the muslin with boiling water, discarding the water.

   Pour the liquid and petals through the muslin-lined colander. When the liquid stops dripping, discard the contents of the muslin.

   Strain the orange and lemon juice and add with the citric acid and sugar to the pan. Warm on a low heat and cook gently to dissolve the sugar; stir and then simmer for a few more minutes. Pour through a sieve into a measuring jug.

Frothy elderflower heads gathered from the hedgerows in early summer.

Unsprayed rose petals pulled from the flower heads in readiness for making cordial.

Elderflower cordial ingredients.

Strip the elderflowers from the heads.

Fill the bottle using a funnel.

3 Once cool, using a funnel fill the bottle, leaving a small gap of 2cm between the top of the liquid and the top of the bottle. Screw the lid down securely.

   Make all summer long. It can be used straight away and will last between 3 and 6 months if kept in the fridge.

To keep long term, pasteurize or freeze in plastic bottles.

CHAPTER 5

Sugar, Spice, Vinegar and All Things Nice: Chutney and Ketchup

. . . .

This chapter concentrates on the store cupboard standbys, guaranteed to bring the simplest cheese board to life, to elevate cold cuts to a feast or to transform a sandwich. These sweet and sour combinations of sugar, spice and vinegar, added to vegetables and fruit, make super delicious condiments for everyday eating.

Chutneys and ketchups are found in most Western kitchen cupboards but, surprisingly, they originated far away on the other side of the world.

WHERE DID THEY COME FROM?

The word chutney or chutnee, originated in India from the Hindi *chatni* or *satni*, meaning a fresh relish prepared with sweet fruits, acid flavourings such as lemon, sour herbs, hot chilli and other spices. According to the *Shorter Oxford English Dictionary* (1989), the word chutney had entered the English language by 1813.

During the Colonial era the British discovered and fell in love with these chutneys. They brought the recipes with them on their return and introduced them back home along with the hot curry dishes that they had also learned to love.

They made chutneys with what was available in more temperate climes, such as apples, quince, pears, pumpkins and marrows, rather than exotic fruits. By this time sugar was readily available and this too was added to the Western

version. What had begun life as a fresh spicy relish or *chatni* became the long-keeping sweet and sour, spicy preserve we know and love. The preserves journeyed on to other colonies to become staples in South Africa and the Caribbean, where they too were made with the local produce.

Since then it has travelled around our 'food-without-borders' twenty-first century, to become popularly served with cheese and curries in many European countries.

The word Ketchup or Catchup entered the English language even earlier, in 1711, probably via the Malay *kichap*, which in turn originated from an Amoy, South-Eastern Chinese dialect word, *kôechiap*, meaning fish brine. This was not unlike the Garum fish sauce so popular in Roman food or the Asian fish sauces we know today.

So how did a Far Eastern fish sauce ever become a sweet and sour vegetable or fruit sauce? Recipes abound in old British cookery books for mushroom, walnut, anchovy and oyster ketchups, but there is no mention of tomato ketchup.

When a ketchup-like tomato concoction finally appeared in the UK and many parts of the Commonwealth it was referred to as tomato or red sauce, rather than ketchup.

In the 1950s the red sauce made and bottled by Heinz, which had made its way into the family store cupboard, was referred to as tomato sauce, even though it had the word 'ketchup' emblazoned across the label. Was this because it was rich and gloopy like sauce, not watery and dark like the 'cook's little helper' ketchups that had once been essential ingredients?

In American English the word 'catsup' appears to have been adopted for fruit sauces such as Apple Catsup, Gooseberry Catsup and Grape Catsup. In these recipes the fruit is cooked with sugar, cider vinegar, onions and

◀ Serve a variety of preserves with cheese: kitchen garden, apricot and almond and apple.

spices. When Henry J. Heinz started manufacturing his now legendary Heinz ketchup in 1876 he introduced it to the world as 'tomato catsup', not ketchup.

As tomato ketchup became increasingly popular in the USA there were 'red sauce wars' between the long-standing rival producers Hunt's and Heinz. To begin with the two manufacturers used different spellings, but Heinz gave in eventually, in part due to a US law declaring 'ketchup' a vegetable when used in a school lunch. Umm … do we consider ketchup to be one of our five a day?

LET'S GET STARTED

Here as in previous chapters there will be master recipes with variations: that is, a basic recipe followed by some suggestions on how to vary it. By using different fruit and vegetables, different spices and additives, but sticking to the same method, the classic apple chutney recipe can become a pear, tamarind and ginger or an apricot, almond and cardamom chutney. Once the basic preserve recipes are mastered, the cook will be able to create an infinity of flavours, ultimately coming up with their own innovative concoctions.

The question I am asked most often in my lessons about a specific preserve is, 'What should I serve it with?' The answer to this is probably everything to start with. That way you will soon discover what it pairs with best. Whatever you do, make sure that a new preserve is not left to stray unused to the back of the cupboard.

Jars, lids and covers

Use upcycled jars wherever possible. Our resources are becoming ever more precious. Discard jars that are cracked or chipped. Lids become damaged over time and may not create a hermetic seal. Therefore, either use cellophane discs brushed with warm water, secured wet side up, with an elastic band, or simply lay a cellophane disc over the mouth of the jar and screw the old lid down over it. This will prevent any bacteria creeping in.

Preserves containing vinegar tend to corrode metal lids unless they have a cardboard, paper or plastic lining. Therefore use a cellophane disc or cut a circle of greaseproof paper to line the lid before sealing jars and bottles when using metal lids.

When making preserves for sale use new jars and lids.

Adding vinegar

All the chutney recipe ingredients include a double quantity of vinegars (for example, 200–400ml of vinegar). Add 200ml of vinegar at the start, keeping back 200ml to add, if and when necessary, as the chutney boils down. How much you use will depend how long and how hard the chutney boils. It will also depend on whether a stainless-steel or aluminium pan is used. Make sure you add just a little vinegar at a time and let that evaporate before adding more. If you use up all the vinegar, it is possible to add a little water to keep the pan moist, but remember to add only a little at a time.

Which vinegar?

As a rule of thumb, use white or red wine vinegars to make chutneys and similar preserves made with Mediterranean and tropical type produce. Use malt, white or cider vinegars and fruit vinegars for preserves made with root vegetables, hard fruits and squashes.

Try to match pale coloured vinegar to pale coloured produce to retain the original colour of the produce and a dark vinegar to dark produce. For example, add apple or white vinegar to gooseberry and rose petal chutney to retain the soft gooseberry green hue, but use sherry or red wine vinegar when added to red onions.

Which sugar?

All sugar is equal when it comes to nutritional value, but sugars vary hugely in colour and flavour. Muscovado is dark brown with a burned caramel flavour. Demerara is golden brown and has a rich caramel taste. When making jam use white granulated sugar for almost everything, unless you would like to create a darker, richer flavour and colour. The more strident flavours and rich colours of chutneys can accommodate the full range of sugars, golden syrup and treacle.

If you have issues with sugar, remember that you are only using a teaspoon or so of preserve to enhance the natural flavours of foods such as bread, cheese, fish, vegetables, salads and meats.

Sugar brings out flavour, balances the tartness of the vinegar and preserves. If you prefer to reduce the quantity of sugar to enjoy your chutneys, you will need to pasteurize the finished jars as the high volume of sugar helps keepability (see Chapter 2). Sweetness drops back quite quickly in a chutney: if you are adding sugar to taste, I advise using the resultant jars quite quickly because, if you keep them for any length of time, the flavours do not mature in the same way.

Fruit and veg

Make chutneys with any combination of fruit, fresh and dried (soaked first) and vegetables. Onions and shallots work well in all savoury preserves. Choose white or red, keeping in mind the colour of the other ingredients. Naturally, if you grow your own, use what you have. Sultanas, raisins and currants work well to add sweetness, flavour and texture. Remember to ring the changes.

Spices and aromatics

Garlic and ginger work well across the board. Try to vary the spices you use and experiment, perhaps choosing a combination of three or four different ones. Your preserves do not have to be hot unless you like them that way. Chilli acts rather like salt: adding just a pinch of chilli enhances the taste of a preserve, bringing out its flavours rather than making it hot.

When using whole spices, such as cinnamon, mace, star anise, cloves and allspice, tie them up in a piece of muslin or put them in a small bag and attach to the pan handle. Seeds such as fennel, coriander, cumin, cardamom, chilli flakes and juniper berries can go directly in the pan with the other ingredients. All ground spices are good.

When adding tamarind syrup, go easy as it is very dark in colour and makes everything black.

Use fresh or dried herbs: dried herbs require long, slow cooking, while finely chopped fresh herbs can be added towards the end.

Long and slow

Chutneys and similar preserves benefit from long, slow cooking as it enhances colour, flavour and texture, and ensures longevity:

1   Put the chopped ingredients in the pan with half the vinegar.
2   Simmer over low heat until everything is soft and looks homogeneous, only adding more vinegar if the chutney looks in danger of drying out. It is possible to add a little water from time to time as necessary to stop the pan from catching, if the ingredients need further cooking.
3   The final chutney should look dense and rich.

Chop your chosen ingredients and put them in the pan.

Simmer until everything is soft.

Chutney should be dense and rich.

Potting

All master recipes include full potting instructions, but to save space 'sundry' recipes do not. Please mark this page.

1 Fill the jars to the base of the neck.
2 Tap the jars on a folded cloth to release any air bubbles that may be trapped around the sides of the jar. If the level of the chutney reduces, top it up again to the base of the neck.
3 Cover the surface with wax discs, shiny side down, and seal the jars with cellophane circles and lids or dampened cellophane circles, secured with an elastic band, if using upcycled jars, or use new lids.
4 Wipe the jar with a clean damp cloth.
5 Put all your dirty utensils in the saucepan. Fill up with *cold water* and leave to stand. All the sticky mess will dissolve away.
6 Label the jars when cool.
7 Keep for 1–3 months before you try it. This kind of chutney improves the longer you keep it. If you can resist eating it, it will keep for years.

Keeping

Traditionally preserves were made during the growing months and consumed in the dead months of winter. This avoided waste in the summer and enhanced eating when fresh produce was scarce in winter.

Preserves, like cheese and wine, mature with age. Although they are difficult to resist, it is best to leave them for three months before you try. The feast of Christmas was and is the time to start opening and enjoying them, but you can eat them straight away if you prefer.

Flavours mature over time: both sweetness and acidity drop back, enriching the flavour of the fruit and vegetables.

A good chutney will keep for a year at least, probably several years, given that it is made with sugar, salt and vinegar and cooked long and slow.

Mother Haywood's apple chutney

This recipe came from a 1940s handwritten cookery book and is described as 'Mother Haywood's apple chutney'. Mother Haywood was the live-in widowed mother of the landlord of a local public house. Post-war, this was an 'honorary' title in many family businesses. The chutney was a favourite in the pub and subsequently became a favourite with many customers. As recipes pass from cook to cook, they take on a new name and a new life. Now is the time to make this your own! You could make it with pears or quinces for a change.

Makes 1.5kg

Ingredients
- 1kg cooking apples, quince or pears
- 500g onions, quartered
- 125g raisins
- 125g sultanas
- 400–500g demerara sugar
- ½ teaspoon cayenne pepper
- ½ teaspoon ground ginger
- ½ teaspoon dry mustard powder
- 2 lumps of stem ginger finely chopped
- 15g salt
- 500ml malt vinegar, plus extra to add as and if the chutney boils down

- Preserving pan
- 4 × 400ml jars
- Pack of jam pot covers and labels

Before you start
- Wash the jars in warm soapy water, rinse and drain. Put in an oven set at 125°C for 20 minutes to sterilize.
- Put the lids in a pan, add enough water to cover, bring to the boil and boil for 5 minutes.

1 Chop the fruit and onions finely; this can be done in a food processor (the original recipe called for a mincer), but take care not to reduce the fruit to a pulp, particularly when using pears, as the chutney needs texture.
2 Put the chopped fruit and onion, raisins, sultanas,

Cooking apples come into their own with apple chutney.

Chop the fruit and onions in a food processor.

Simmer the ingredients for 60–90 minutes.

Add extra vinegar, if necessary, as the chutney boils down.

Fill warm, clean jars to the base of the neck.

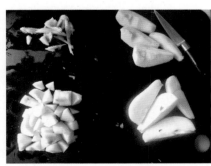

Chop pears by hand as they can go mushy in the blender.

Apricot, almond and cardamom chutney ingredients.

sugar, cayenne, mustard, ginger, salt and 500ml vinegar in the pan and simmer for 60–90 minutes over low to medium heat.

3 Stir regularly to make sure the sugar does not catch, adding extra vinegar, if necessary, as the chutney boils down.

Turn off the heat and let the chutney settle for 10 minutes.

4 Stir and pack into warm, clean jars. Fill to the base of the neck.

Tap the jars on a folded cloth to release any air bubbles that may be trapped around the sides of the jar. If the level of the chutney reduces, top it up again to the base of the neck.

5 Cover the surface with wax discs (shiny side down) and seal the jars with cellophane circles and lids or dampened cellophane circles secured with an elastic band, if using upcycled jars, or use new lids. Wipe the jar with a clean damp cloth.

Put all your dirty utensils in the saucepan and fill up with *cold water*. Leave to stand and all the sticky mess will dissolve away.

Label jars when cool.

Keep for 1–3 months before you try it. This kind of chutney improves the longer you keep it and will keep for years.

Variations

Pear, tamarind, cardamom and ginger chutney

- Omit the apples, cayenne and mustard
- Add 1kg pears, peeled, cored and chopped by hand
- 1 tablespoon tamarind paste
- Vary whole spices to create new flavours
- 1 egg-sized piece of root ginger, grated
- Crushed seeds of 9 cardamom pods
- Retain all other ingredients and proceed as per apple chutney

Apricot, almond and cardamom chutney

- Omit the apples, ginger, cayenne and dried fruit
- Replace with 500g of soaked, dried and drained pitted apricots
- 100g flaked almonds
- 10 cardamom pods, crushed in a mortar and pestle, chaff discarded, and seeds crushed
- Retain all other ingredients and proceed as per apple chutney

Kitchen garden chutney: butternut squash and tomato

This is a great recipe to use up all kinds of root vegetables and squashes through the growing year. Its lovely tomato-red hue makes a pleasant addition to cold cuts. When using butternut squash it will need long slow cooking. Remember to taste the chutney to make sure the vegetable cubes are tender unless, of course, you like more of a pickle finish. There is no need to peel marrow and courgettes, but pumpkins and squashes will need peeling.

Makes 1.5kg

Ingredients

- 500g ripe tomatoes
- 1kg butternut squash, marrow, pumpkin, celeriac, carrot, sweet potato or sliced courgettes
- 500g onions, roughly chopped
- 400g demerara sugar
- 1 teaspoon salt
- 1 thumb-sized lump fresh ginger root, peeled and finely chopped
- 5 garlic cloves, finely chopped
- ½ nutmeg freshly grated
- 1 level teaspoon of cinnamon
- 400ml cider vinegar plus 200ml extra

- Preserving pan
- 4 × 350–400ml jars
- Pack of jam pot covers and labels

Before you start

- Wash the jars in warm soapy water, rinse and drain. Put in an oven set at 125°c for 20 minutes to sterilize.
- Put the lids in a pan, add enough water to cover, bring to the boil and boil for 5 minutes.

1 To skin the tomatoes, score at the widest part, one way and then the other, then plunge into a bowl of freshly boiled water for 5 minutes.
2 Spear one of the tomatoes with a fork and try lifting a corner of the skin.
3 If it peels away easily, pour away the water. If not, return the tomato to the water and leave for a few more minutes and repeat. Peel all the tomatoes.
4 Roughly chop the tomatoes.
5 Peel and deseed the butternut squash and cut into

Kitchen garden chutney ingredients.

Score the tomatoes all the way round and immerse in boiling water.

When the skin starts to lift, peel the tomatoes.

Roughly chop the skinned tomatoes.

Cut the butternut squash into cubes.

Put all the ingredients in a pan and bring to the boil.

After simmering for 90 minutes the chutney should be a rich reddish brown.

Transfer the chutney to warmed jars.

Store in a cool, dark cupboard.

1cm cubes.

6 Put all the ingredients in the pan.

7 Bring slowly to the boil.

8 Simmer for 90 minutes, stirring from time to time. The butternut squash should be tender, and the chutney should look dense and a rich reddish brown. Top up with extra vinegar as necessary. If the chutney dries out too much, or looks in danger of catching, add a little water from time to time.

9 Transfer to the warmed jars.

10 Cover the surface of the chutney with a waxed disc. Wipe the jar with a clean damp cloth.

11 Seal at once with lids or dampened cellophane discs and elastic bands.

Label when cool and store for 1–3 months in a cool, dark cupboard before opening.

Keeps for 12 months or more.

Variations

Triple ginger and butternut squash chutney

- Use butternut squash cut into cubes. Omit the tomato, garlic, cinnamon and nutmeg. Add 2 lumps of stem ginger, finely chopped, and 1 teaspoon of ground ginger to the finely chopped ginger root and other ingredients. Proceed as per the recipe above for kitchen garden chutney.

Spiced root vegetable chutney

- Instead of the butternut squash, use 1kg of mixed root vegetables (carrot, celeriac, parsnip and turnip), cut into bite-sized cubes. Add with the tomato and onion, 200g raisins and 1 teaspoon each of ground ginger, chilli flakes and cumin (instead of the ginger root, nutmeg and cinnamon).

- Retain all other ingredients and proceed as per the recipe above for kitchen garden chutney.

SUNDRY CHUTNEY RECIPES

Sweet chilli tomato jam

This sticky, delicious, sweetly spiced tomato jam makes the perfect match for any type of cured cold meat or cheese. Its beautiful translucent tomato red colour cries out to be served spread on toasted crusty bread or sourdough, topped with fresh ricotta or goat's cheese, for breakfast, as a starter or a snack at any time of day.

Ingredients

- 1kg ripe tomatoes, skinned. If preferred, you can use 4 × 400g tins whole plum tomatoes, drained
- 3 or 4 fresh chillies; discard seeds and chop finely
- 1 large lump of fresh ginger, finely chopped or grated
- ½ head of garlic, finely chopped
- Finely grated zest and juice of 2 lemons
- 300–400g of granulated sugar

- Preserving pan
- 4 × 250ml jars and lids
- Pack of jam pot covers and labels

Before you start

- Wash the jars in warm soapy water, rinse and drain. Put in an oven set at 125°C for 20 minutes to sterilize.
- Put the lids in a pan, add enough water to cover, bring to the boil and boil for 5 minutes.

1 Either chop the skinned tomatoes or break them up by squeezing them through your fingers into the preserving pan
2 Slit the chillies lengthways and scrape out the seeds using a teaspoon.
3 Finely chop the chillies and garlic.
4 Grate the ginger.
5 Grate the zest and juice the lemon.
6 Add these and the sugar to the pan.
7 Set over medium heat and stir until the sugar has

Sweet chilli tomato jam ingredients.

Chop or break up the skinned tomatoes.

Scrape out all the chilli seeds.

Chop the chillies and garlic

Grate the ginger and zest, and juice the lemon.

Place the ingredients in the pan and add the sugar.

Cook the tomato mixture until it thickens. It is ready when you scrape the spoon across the base of the pan and it leaves a trail.

Pour the jam into sterilized jars.

dissolved.

8 When the tomato mixture starts to simmer, increase the heat to high until the water content of the tomatoes evaporates and the tomato jam becomes thick and translucent. This can take anything from half an hour up to an hour or even longer, depending on the water content of the tomatoes. It must really look like a jam; the tomatoes must cook down to a smooth sticky pulp.

As the tomatoes boil down, they are liable to stick to the bottom of the pan: it is essential to stir the mixture regularly and stir constantly toward the end of the cooking time to avoid catching. Add a little water from time to time as necessary. When the jam is ready, slide the pan off the heat and leave to settle for 10 minutes.

9 Stir well and transfer to a large jug. Pour into the sterile jars or fill using a spoon and jam funnel. Tap the jars on a folded cloth to level the contents and top up as necessary.

10 Cover with waxed paper.

11 Seal whilst still hot with lids or cellophane discs. Label when cool.

12 Leave for a month before opening and taste. It should keep for at least a year, perhaps two.

Aromatic gooseberry and rose petal chutney

This pretty but punchy sweet and sour chutney is a perfect accompaniment for oily fish, such as mackerel or salmon. It goes well with goat's cheeses and adds an unusual touch to a cheese sandwich or a toasty.

Cook over low heat to help retain the pale green colour of the gooseberries.

Aromatic gooseberry and rose petal chutney ingredients.

Makes approximately 1kg

Ingredients

- 1 teaspoon cardamom pods
- 400g onions, chopped finely
- 1 large cooking apple
- 1 level teaspoon coriander
- 1 level teaspoon cumin
- 500g gooseberries, topped and tailed
- 300g granulated sugar
- 10g sea salt
- 100ml cider vinegar
- 3 handfuls of pink or white rose petals.

- Preserving pan
- 4 × 250ml jars and lids
- Pack of jam pot covers and labels

Before you start

- Wash the jars in warm soapy water, rinse and drain. Put in an oven set at 125°C for 20 minutes to sterilize.
- Put the lids in a pan, add enough water to cover, bring to the boil and boil for 5 minutes.

1   Put the cardamom pods in a pestle and mortar and crush to release the seeds. Pick out the chaff and discard, then lightly crush the seeds.
2   Put a large heavy-based pan on low heat. Add enough extra-virgin olive oil to cover the base of the pan. Add the onion and apple, cook until warmed through.

Make sure the onions don't brown.

3   Add the spices and cook until the onion is tender and fragrant. Add 2 tablespoons of cold water to stop the onions browning.
4   Add the gooseberries, sugar and salt, Stir over low heat until the sugar has dissolved. Add half the vinegar and cook until the liquid evaporates, and the chutney is thick and pulpy, say 25 minutes. Then add the rose petals.

When the chutney is thick and pulpy, add the rose petals.

5   Cook for 10 more minutes. Add extra vinegar if the chutney dries out too much.

6   Leave to stand for 10 minutes.

7   Stir and spoon into clean, warm jars. Fill to the base of the neck. To complete, *see* the instructions above for 'Potting'.

Cook all the ingredients for another 10 minutes.

Fill the jars to the base of the neck.

Spiced mango chutney with cardamom.

Spiced mango chutney with cardamom

Use pawpaw, papaya, pineapple, prickly pears, peaches, apricots, persimmon or other exotic fruit. Regulate the heat of this chutney by adding more chilli flakes or using less. This is great to serve with curries and other spicy Asian foods. Omit the chilli for a rounded aromatic preserve.

Makes 1kg

Ingredients

- 4 ripe mangoes, stoned, peeled and chopped
- 20g root ginger, finely grated
- 1 onion, finely chopped
- 5 cardamom pods, crushed, chaff removed and seeds ground
- 1 teaspoon turmeric
- 1 teaspoon cumin
- 1 teaspoon chilli flakes
- 100g golden raisins, softened in boiling water for 5 minutes and drained
- 100g demerara sugar
- 100ml white wine vinegar

- Preserving pan
- 4 × 250ml jars and lids
- Pack of jam pot covers and labels

Before you start

- Wash the jars in warm soapy water, rinse and drain. Put in an oven set at 125°C for 20 minutes to sterilize.
- Put the lids in a pan, add enough water to cover, bring to the boil and boil for 5 minutes.

1   Cut the mango in half, remove the stone, peel and chop into medium-sized pieces.

2   Put in a heavy-based preserving pan with the spices, soaked raisins and sugar. Cook over low heat until the sugar dissolves. Cook for a further 30–45 minutes, stirring from time to time, making sure that the juice does not evaporate completely, and the chutney is soft.

3   Add the vinegar and continue cooking until it evaporates and the chutney looks dense.

4   Turn off the heat, rest for 10 minutes, stir well and fill the jars to the base of the neck. To complete, *see* the instructions above for 'Potting' on page 76.

Plum and red onion chutney

This rich, dark red plum preserve is a roller coaster of hot and aromatic spicy flavour, perfect for cheese toasties, egg on toast, cooked breakfast, cold meats and a classic cheese board.

Makes 750ml

Ingredients
- 750g plums, pitted weight
- 350g red onions
- 100g sultanas
- 1 teaspoon chilli flakes
- 10g whole ginger, crushed
- 10g salt
- 350g muscovado sugar
- 1 teaspoon ground turmeric
- 1 teaspoon ground coriander
- 1 teaspoon dry mustard powder
- 400ml cider or wine vinegar

- Preserving pan
- 3 × 300ml sterile jars and lids
- Pack of jam pot covers and labels

Before you start
- Wash the jars in warm soapy water, rinse and drain. Put in an oven set at 125°C for 20 minutes to sterilize.
- Put the lids in a pan, add enough water to cover, bring to the boil and boil for 5 minutes.

1. Using a mincer or food processor, carefully chop the onions, the pitted plums and the sultanas.
2. Put the prepared plums, onions and sultanas in a pan with the chilli flakes, crushed ginger, salt, sugar and other spices. Add half the vinegar, cover with a lid, and bring to simmering point. Cook for 2 hours on low heat. Stir regularly during this time, adding extra vinegar if necessary as it boils down.
3. When the chutney has boiled down and thickened, switch off and rest for 10 minutes.
4. While still hot, decant the chutney into a clean jug and fill the jars to the base of the neck. Wipe with a clean cloth. To complete, *see* the instructions above for 'Potting' on page 76.

Plum and red onion chutney ingredients.

Chop the onions, plums and sultanas in a food processor.

Cook for 2 hours on low heat, stirring regularly.

Aromatic rhubarb and red onion chutney

The combination of these two ingredients makes a glorious purple preserve, scented with cinnamon and star anise and textured with strands of rhubarb.

Be adventurous and experiment with all kinds of fruit and vegetable. You will be delighted at the results.

Ingredients

- 500g rhubarb
- 250g red onions quartered
- 250g demerara sugar
- 1 tablespoon chopped stem ginger in syrup
- 75g golden raisins or sultanas
- 1 star anise
- 1 cinnamon stick
- 1 teaspoon cardamom pods crushed, chaff discarded and seeds crushed
- 10g salt
- 250ml malt vinegar, plus 250ml to use as the chutney boils down (you may not need it all)

- 4 × 250g or 2 × 500g jars and lids
- Small drawstring bag or piece of muslin for whole spices
- Pack of jam pot covers and labels

1. Cut the rhubarb into 1cm chunks. Chop the quartered onion finely; this can be done in a food processor, but take care not to reduce the onion to a pulp as the chutney must have texture.
2. Tie the cinnamon and star anise into a bag and tie this to your pan handle.
3. Put the chopped rhubarb and onion, dried fruit, sugar, chopped ginger, the crushed cardamom seeds, salt and 250ml vinegar in the pan and simmer for 60–90 minutes over low to medium heat. Stir regularly to make sure the sugar does not burn, adding extra vinegar as necessary as the chutney boils down.
4. Turn off the heat and let the chutney settle. Discard the spice bag.
5. Stir and pack into warm, clean jars to the base of the neck. Wipe with a clean cloth. To complete, *see* the instructions on page 76 for 'Potting'.

Red onion marmalade with brandy

Ingredients

- 1kg red onions
- ½ head garlic
- 50ml extra-virgin olive oil
- ½ teaspoon chilli flakes and ½ teaspoon ground cinnamon
- 10g salt
- 1 tablespoon shredded sage leaves
- 100g muscovado sugar
- 125ml sherry vinegar
- 125ml sherry or red wine
- 1 tablespoon brandy

- Preserving pan
- 4 × 250g or 2 × 500g jars
- Pack of jam pot covers and labels

1. Slice the onions finely and chop the garlic.
2. Put the olive oil in the preserving pan, add the onions, garlic, spices, salt and sage. Simmer gently until the onions start to wilt. Add a tablespoon of cold water if they start to catch.
3. Add the sugar, increase the heat and stir until the sugar has dissolved. Continue to cook until the onion has a melting texture and starts to caramelize.
4. Add the vinegar and sherry, stir well and simmer until almost evaporated, say 45 minutes.
5. Stir in the brandy.
6. Turn off the heat and let the chutney settle for 10 minutes.
7. Stir and pack into warm, clean jars. Fill to the base of the neck. Wipe with a clean cloth. To complete, *see* the instructions on page 76 for 'Potting'.

Red onion marmalade with brandy.

KETCHUP

This section covers the ketchup we all know and love, the tomato ketchup, which some call tomato sauce and others affectionately refer to as Tommy K. The lesser-known plum and mushroom variations are included here, too, and like their celebrated big brother make a great instant statement on the side of a plate. They are also a useful ingredient to have in the cupboard to add to casseroles, stews, potted meats, stir fries, cheese on toast, baguettes, panini and sandwiches, indeed anything that needs a bit of sweet and sour pizzazz.

I have cheekily also included a recipe for tomato passata, which, although not strictly a preserve, is the best and simplest way ever to preserve a glut of tomatoes. It will need to be pasteurized.

Tomato ketchup

Makes 500ml

Ingredients
- 500g very ripe tomatoes
- 10g fine sea salt
- 1 small cooking apple
- 50g onion or shallot
- 15g sugar
- 50ml vinegar
- Good pinch each of ground white pepper, ground clove and mace

- Large pan with lid
- 2 × 250ml bottles and lids or Kilner jars and seals

Before you start
- Wash the bottle, bottles or jars in warm soapy water, rinse and drain. Put in an oven set at 125°C for 20 minutes to sterilize.
- Put the cap, caps or seals in a pan, add enough water to cover, bring to the boil and boil for 5 minutes.

1 Slice the tomatoes and lay them out on a shallow dish, sprinkle with salt and leave for an hour.
2 Quarter and core the apple and chop. Peel and chop the onion. Put the apple and onion in a pan with the sugar, vinegar and spices and bring to the boil on low heat.
3 Add the salted tomatoes and stir well, cover with a lid.

The basis of home-grown tomato ketchup.

Slice the tomatoes and sprinkle with salt.

Bring the other ingredients to the boil at a low heat.

Add the tomatoes, stir and cover.

4 Simmer on very low heat for 1–2 hours. Watch and stir regularly.

5 Puree using a mouli-légumes.

7 Wash the pan and return the puree to it. Simmer, covered, for 30 minutes.

8 Watch and stir. The ketchup should have a pouring consistency. If too thick, add a little water; if too thin, cook for a little longer.

   While still hot, decant the hot sauce into a clean jug and fill the hot sterile bottles or jars with the help of a funnel, leaving a 1–2cm gap at the top. Seal and label when cool.

Puree with a mouli-légumes.

The ketchup should have a pouring consistency.

Fill the bottles or jars with the help of a funnel or jug.

Mushroom ketchup

Anyone familiar with the countryside and who loves walking will know never to go out in early autumn without a paper bag and a penknife in their pocket. This is field mushroom time, but please, unless you know your mushrooms from your toadstools, don't attempt to pick them. Find someone who does and go out with them. If, in doubt, go without.

Field mushrooms, however, are easy to spot once you know what you are doing. Early morning is the best time for mushrooming and there is no finer treat than returning from an autumn walk and cooking a few mushrooms for breakfast. In a good year it is possible to find stacks of field mushrooms and that is when this recipe is useful.

As with most fresh produce, it is best to pick it on a dry day, but if the mushrooms are wet you will need to be deal with them straight away. Spread them out on a clean dry cloth and set to work.

Making a ketchup is a simple and useful way to preserve rich pickings. Serve with a cooked breakfast or scrambled eggs. Add to quiches, tarts, pies, stuffing, casseroles and stews.

You can also use this recipe to make beetroot ketchup.

Freshly picked mushrooms.

Ingredients

- 500g field or other open mushrooms or grated beetroot
- 10g fine sea salt
- 1 shallot, sliced
- 1 clove garlic, sliced
- Small pinch ground allspice
- Small pinch ground clove
- Small pinch ground cayenne
- Small pinch ground coriander
- Handful roughly chopped parsley
- 50ml malt vinegar

- Large pan and lid
- 2 or 3 × 250ml bottles or Kilner type jars

Before you start

- Wash bottles or jars in hot soapy water, rinse and put on a baking tray in a pre-heated oven at 125°C for 20 minutes to sterilize.
- Simmer lids and seals in boiling water for 5 minutes and drain on a clean cloth.

1. Wipe the mushrooms, do not immerse in water. Trim the stalks and break into pieces or chop roughly. Put the prepared mushrooms in an earthenware or stainless-steel pan, sprinkle with salt and leave overnight or for at least 8 hours.

   After this time, add the sliced onion and garlic, the spices and parsley.

   Cover with the pan lid, put on low heat and simmer for 30 minutes, stirring from time to time. Add a little water if necessary.

   Then puree the cooked mushroom mixture in a blender or with a stick blender or mouli-légumes.

   Return the puree to the pan, adding the vinegar and bring back to simmering point. Cook for a further 10 minutes.

2. The ketchup should have a thick pouring consistency. If too thick, slacken with a little water; if too runny, cook a little longer with the lid off. For a luxurious finish, add a tablespoon of dry sherry or Marsala wine.

3. While still hot, decant the hot sauce into a clean jug and fill the hot sterile bottles or jars with the help of a funnel, leaving a 1–2cm gap at the top. To complete, *see* the instructions above for 'Potting' on page 76. Label when cool.

For something special, add a tablespoon of dry sherry or Marsala wine.

Plum ketchup

Anyone who has a plum tree in their garden will welcome a new way of using up the harvest. In a good year it is not unusual to find yourself ankle-deep in windfalls by late summer.

Add plum ketchup to casseroles, stir fries and stews where you would normally use tomato ketchup, Worcester sauce, soy or tomato concentrate. Use as you would any other ketchup.

You can also use this recipe for gooseberries, elderberries and apples.

Makes 750ml

Ingredients

- 350g plums, pitted weight
- 500g onions
- 75g sultanas
- 1 teaspoon chilli flakes
- 10g whole ginger, crushed
- 300ml cider vinegar
- 10g salt
- 100–150g sugar to taste
- ½ teaspoon star anise
- ½ teaspoon ground coriander
- ½ teaspoon Chinese five spice

- 2 or 3 × 300ml swing-top bottles or Kilner type jars

Add the chilli flakes and crushed ginger to the prepared plums, onions and sultanas.

Pureeing the mix in a mouli-légumes until only the debris remains can create quite a mess.

Return the puree to the pan.

Extra sugar can be added if preferred.

Before you start

- Wash the bottles or jars in hot soapy water, rinse and put on a baking tray in a pre-heated oven at 125°c and heat for 20 minutes.
- Simmer lids and seals in boiling water for 5 minutes and drain on a clean cloth.

1 Pit the plums and slice the onions. Put the prepared plums, onions and sultanas in a pan with the chilli flakes and crushed ginger. Add the vinegar, cover with a lid and bring to simmering point and cook for 30 minutes on low heat or until tender.

2 Put the plum and onion mix in a mouli-légumes. It is quite a messy job and best done over a bowl in the sink.

3 Grind the pulp until only the debris is left behind.

4 Then return the puree to the pan.

5 Have the salt, 100g sugar and remaining spices ready to add.

6 Add the prepared ingredients

7 Stir and cook with the lid on for 15 minutes. Taste for sweetness and add extra sugar if liked. The ketchup should have a thick pouring consistency. If too thick, slacken with a little water; if too runny, cook a little longer with the lid off.

While still hot decant the hot sauce into a clean jug and fill the hot sterile bottles or Kilner jars with the help of a funnel, leaving a gap at the top. To complete, *see* the instructions on page 76 for 'Potting'. Label when cool.

Tomato passata

This may be an interloper when talking about ketchup and sauces, but who could resist including this here? It's hardly a 'sugar and spice' preserve, but it's just so useful.

This is the classic tomato sauce at the heart of so much Italian cooking. The essential ingredient of spaghetti al pomodoro. If you grow tomatoes and are inundated in summer, it is a simple way to preserve them without the addition of either sugar or vinegar.

You will, of course, need to pasteurize the sauce if you want to keep it for any length of time. Some cooks like to add a teaspoon of sugar to their passata, others do not – the choice is yours.

Ingredients

- 1.5kg tomatoes, cut into quarters
- 1 large onion, roughly chopped
- 2 cloves garlic
- Salt and sugar to taste
- A few sprigs of basil

- Large pan and lid
- 3 × 350ml or 500ml bottles or jars

Before you start

- Wash bottles or jars in hot soapy water, rinse, drain and put on a baking tray in a pre-heated oven at 125°C for 20 minutes to sterilize.
- Simmer lids and seals in boiling water for 5 minutes and drain on a clean cloth.

1. Quarter the tomatoes.
2. Roughly chop the onion.
3. Add to a large saucepan with the garlic and basil.
4. Cook on low for 30 minutes, then discard the basil.
5. Put through a mouli-légumes or liquidizer and sieve the passata.
6. Taste for salt and sugar, then bring back to a simmer and cook for another 30 minutes.
7. While still hot, decant the hot sauce into a clean jug and fill the hot sterile bottles or jars with the help of a funnel, leaving a gap at the top. To complete, *see* the instructions above for 'Potting'.

This is a recipe that will need pasteurizing. For full details and illustrations, *see* page 23.

When the jars are cold, dry, label and store them in a cool dark place. Do not open until after 1 month. Once open store in the fridge and use within 6 months.

Freshly picked tomatoes in from the garden.

Place the tomatoes, onion, garlic and basil in a large saucepan.

Cook for 30 minutes, remove the basil, and puree using a mouli-légumes.

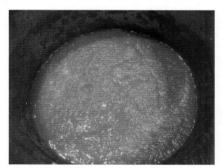

Taste for salt and sugar before cooking for another 30 minutes.

Ladle the passata into jars and bottles using a funnel.

CHAPTER 6

In a Pickle: Pickles in Vinegar, Wine and Extra-Virgin Olive Oil

· ·

There may be some confusion between vinegar bath pickles and lacto-fermented pickles, which you will find in the next chapter.

What of the pickle in this chapter – the whole fruit or vegetable, preserved in vinegar? Here you will find the most iconic, ubiquitous, dearly beloved British pickled onion, once the constant of every English public house bar. Or perhaps the pinnacle of perfection, the final flourish to a ploughman's lunch – crusty bread, creamy butter, crumbly, jowl-teasing Cheddar cheese and pickled onions. No frills are required: brine and spiced malt vinegar are all it takes. Traditionally pickling was not a job for the women of the house: pickling was a man's preserve. Other stealthy pickles of this genre include red cabbage, beetroot and eggs. Then there is the vibrant, turmeric-rich piccalilli with its runner bean and cauliflower variations.

If you are looking for a gherkin recipe, go straight to pickles and ferments in Chapter 7. Cucumbers pickle best in the lactic acid produced by salt brine rather than in vinegar.

Over and above the pickled vegetables there are the elegant fruit pickles: figs, damsons and plums to serve with smoked game and duck. There is also a pickled gooseberry variation that goes well with oily fish such as mackerel and salmon.

For those who enjoy a more sophisticated, subtle pickle, there is an array of Italian antipasto pickles preserved in vinegar, wine, water and extra-virgin olive oil, spiked with herbs and garlic. Last but not least, there are baby onions in balsamic vinegar.

Traditional pickles, cured in pure vinegar and/or sugar, will keep indefinitely when enclosed in sterile jars. Subtler concoctions, containing small quantities or no sugar, and mixes of vinegar, water, wine and oil, such as the recipes for baby peppers and asparagus spears, require further processing and need to be pasteurized. Where this step is essential, pasteurization instructions are an integral part of the recipe and will also be found, with illustrations, on page 23.

PICKLES FOR COLD MEATS, GAME, PIES AND CHEESES

Winter's Farm pickled onions

This recipe is for a no-nonsense, British pub-counter pickled onion. If you prefer a little sweetness, add sugar (*see* below) or use wine or cider vinegar, rather than malt vinegar.

If you do not want to go to the trouble of making your own spiced vinegar, as described here, you can buy it ready-made in 2-litre bottles from most supermarkets

Use this recipe to pickle shredded red cabbage and beetroot. These should first be roasted and allowed to cool, or grated raw.

◄ A trio of Italian pickles, baby peppers, balsamic onions and asparagus.

Pour boiling water over the shallots to loosen the skins.

For the spiced vinegar, once brought to the boil, the vinegar and spices should be left to stand and cool.

Once brined, the shallots are drained, rinsed and dried, then packed into jars.

Top up the jars with cooled spiced vinegar.

Ready to grace any pub counter.

Ingredients

- 50g salt
- 500g shallots or pickling onions

For the spiced vinegar

- 500ml malt or white wine vinegar
- 12g whole mixed pickling spice (or mix a small piece of cinnamon, chilli, coriander seeds, cloves, allspice, mace, white peppercorns and a pinch of cayenne)
- 50g light muscovado sugar (optional if you like a slightly sweet and sour onion)

- 1 × 500ml jar or 2 × 250ml jars and lids
- Cellophane or greaseproof paper circles and labels

Before you start

- Wash jars in hot soapy water, rinse, invert and put on a baking tray in a pre-heated oven at 125°C for 20 minutes to sterilize.
- Simmer lids or wires and seals in boiling water for 5 minutes and drain on a clean cloth.

1 To make peeling the shallots easier, put them in a large bowl. Pour boiling water over them and leave for a few minutes. Drain and peel.
2 To make brine, mix the salt with the water.
   Put the peeled shallots in a large bowl, add the brine to cover and leave for 24 hours.
3 Meanwhile put the vinegar and spices in a large non-metallic bowl and stand the bowl over a pan of water. Bring to the boil (add sugar if using) and then take off the heat source. Leave to stand for 2 hours to infuse, then strain into a jug.
4 When ready to pickle the onions; drain, rinse in cold water and dry them carefully.
5 Pack the onions into a jar or jars, pushing them down with the handle of a wooden spoon.
6 Top up the jars with the cooled spiced vinegar, adding the whole spices if liked. Tap the sides of the jar to release any air bubbles that may be trapped around the sides of the jar.
7 Cover the mouth of the jar with greaseproof paper or cellophane discs, and seal with a screw-top lid. Store the jars in a cool dark cupboard until required.

Wait 1–3 months before tasting. These should keep at least 12 months.

Pickled figs

This elegant pickle enhances the flavour of smoked meats, particularly smoked duck, game and poultry. Try serving with pâtés and terrines for a change.

It is important to pickle the fruit before it is fully ripe, when it has coloured up but is still firm, otherwise you will end up with soft, mushy pickles.

Use this recipe for damsons, greengages, small plums and gooseberries.

Pickled figs ingredients.

Ingredients

- 500g firm, just underripe, small figs, damsons, greengages, small plums or gooseberries (plums and damsons need piercing)
- 60g granulated sugar
- 300ml white wine vinegar
- ½ cinnamon bark
- 1 star anise
- Small piece ginger root

- 1 × 500–750ml jar and lid

Before you start

- Wash jar in hot soapy water, rinse, invert and put on a baking tray in a pre-heated oven at 125°C for 20 minutes to sterilize.
- Simmer lid and seal in boiling water for 5 minutes and drain on a clean cloth.

Remove the fruit from the syrup as soon as it comes to the boil.

1 To make the syrup, combine the white wine vinegar and sugar with the ginger, the piece of cinnamon stick and star anise in a small pan. Bring to simmering point over low heat and simmer for 5 minutes.

Drop the fruit into the simmering syrup and leave until the syrup comes back to the boil, then remove the fruit quickly with a slotted spoon and put in the sterilized cooled jar.

2 Leave the syrup until completely cold and pour it over the fruit and add the aromatics.

Cover the neck of the jar with a cellophane or greaseproof circle and screw down the lid.

When the syrup is cold, pour it over the fruit.

Label and store in the dark for at least a month, for best results, before opening. It will keep until the following season.

Spring vegetable piccalilli

Piccalilli is a traditional favourite that can be varied according to season and taste. This version uses small, young new season vegetables, but you can also make it later in the season with bite-sized pieces of mature vegetables, such as cauliflower, cucumber, green tomatoes and peppers.

Serve with curries and other spicy dishes, bread and cheese, or stir into a frittata or salad.

Spring vegetable piccalilli ingredients.

Blanch the vegetables in batches, depending on the cooking time needed.

Chop the onions and fry over low heat. Make sure they don't brown and, when tender, add the blanched vegetables.

Makes 1kg

Ingredients

- 800g mixed summer vegetables (e.g. 200g young shelled broad beans, 200g asparagus or green beans, 100g young celery, 100g baby carrots, 200g baby courgettes or shelled peas)
- 400g onions
- 1 tablespoon mustard seeds
- 1 tablespoon coriander seeds
- 200g demerara sugar to taste
- 200ml wine vinegar
- 1 scant tablespoon cornflour
- 1 tablespoon turmeric
- 1 tablespoon mustard powder
- A bunch of mint or other fresh herbs, finely chopped
- Salt
- Extra-virgin olive oil

- Preserving pan
- 4 × 250g jars or 2 × 500g jars or 1 × 1-litre jar and lids
- Pack of jam papers

Before you start

- Wash jars in hot soapy water, rinse and put on a baking tray in a pre-heated oven at 125°C for 20 minutes to sterilize.
- Submerge lids and seals in boiling water for 5 minutes and drain on a clean cloth.

1 Clean the vegetables and divide into bite-sized pieces, keeping each type separate.
2 Blanch the vegetables in batches according to cooking time in boiling salted water until just tender. Drain and refresh in iced water to help retain their crispness. Drain and spread out to dry on a dry, clean tea towel.
3 Chop the onions finely.
4 Put a large, heavy-based pan or preserving pan on low heat, add enough extra-virgin olive oil to cover the base, add the onion, mustard and coriander seed and cook for about 10 minutes, stirring until tender. Do not brown. Add the sugar and stir constantly until dissolved.
5 Stir the blanched vegetables into the onion mix and add half the vinegar and cook for a few minutes.
6 Have the vinegar, cornflour, turmeric and mustard powder ready.

7 Mix to a paste with half the remaining vinegar.

8 Stir this into the pickle until it thickens slightly. If the mix is on the dry side add the remaining vinegar. Keep stirring. Taste for salt, though it may not be needed as the vegetables were salted when blanched.

9 Stir in the chopped herbs and leave to settle for 10 minutes.

10 Stir and pack into warm, clean jars, fill to the base of the neck.

Tap the jars on a folded cloth to release any air bubbles that may be trapped around the sides of the jar. If the level of the pickle reduces, top it up again to the base of the neck.

Cover the surface with wax discs (shiny side down) and seal the jars with cellophane circles and lids, or dampened cellophane circles secured with an elastic band when using upcycled jars, or use new lids.

Wipe the jar with a clean damp cloth.

Put all the dirty utensils in the saucepan and fill with *cold water*. Leave to stand and all the sticky mess will dissolve away.

Label when cool.

Keep for 1–3 months before you try it. This kind of chutney improves the longer you keep it and will keep for years.

Variations

Spicy Cauliflower Piccalilli

- Omit the 800g of spring vegetables and the fresh herbs.
- Add 700g cauliflower, 100g sultanas, 1 teaspoon chilli flakes.
- Retain all other ingredients and proceed as per spring vegetable piccalilli: add the sultanas and the chilli flakes to the onion with the cauliflower at step 5.

Runner bean mustard pickle

- Omit the 800g of spring vegetables, the coriander seeds and the fresh herbs.
- Add 800g of young runner beans, thinly sliced, 100g golden raisins and a tablespoon of black mustard seeds.
- Retain all other ingredients and proceed as per spring vegetable piccalilli: add the black mustard seeds along with the yellow ones at step 4, to cook with the onion.

Mix the cornflour, turmeric, mustard powder and half the vinegar to a paste.

Stir the paste into the pickle.

Serve spring vegetable piccalilli with curries and other spicy dishes, bread and cheese, or stir into a frittata or salad.

ANTIPASTO PICKLES

Makes 2 × 300ml jars

Anyone who has experienced a traditional *alimentari* or grocer's shop in Italy will have been drawn by the giant, colourful, eye-catching jars of layered *sott'olio* and *sott'aceto* vegetables pickled in oil or vinegar.

The surrounding shelves are stacked with diminutive jars crammed with the likes of olives or artichokes, onions, carrots, aubergines and peppers.

They are easy and fun to make at home (although baby artichokes may be difficult to source outside of Italy), they keep well and are great to have to hand to add to cured meats, salamis and cheeses for the starter feast the Italians call antipasto. They are also delicious served with grilled and boiled meats.

Be warned, it is essential to pasteurize when making to keep (*see* page 23).

Italian balsamic pickled onions (Cipolline al aceto balsamico)

If the classic pickled onion is not for you, try these subtle, Italian, sweet and sour balsamic pickled gems. Don't use your Modena estate-bottled *aceto balsamico*, but don't use the cheap supermarket variety either. Seggiano, age certified, is a good-quality, middle of the road choice.

Ingredients

- 500g pearl onions
- 200ml red wine
- 200ml balsamic vinegar
- 150ml extra-virgin olive oil
- 20g coarse sea salt

- 2 × 300ml jars
- Cellophane or greaseproof paper circles and labels

Before you start

- Wash jars in hot soapy water, rinse, invert and put on a baking tray in a pre-heated oven at 125°C for 20 minutes to sterilize.
- Submerge lids and seals in boiling water for 5 minutes and drain on a clean cloth.

1 Trim the root end of the onions and immerse in boiling water and leave for an hour. This makes them easier to peel.
2 Put the wine, balsamic vinegar, 1 small wine glass of extra-virgin olive oil and coarse salt in a large pan and bring to simmering point over low heat.
3 Increase the heat to medium, add the onions, bring back to the boil and simmer for 1 minute.

Once boiled and left for an hour, the onions are easier to peel.

Add the onions to the vinegar mix and bring to the boil, simmering for just 1 minute.

4 Switch off and drain immediately, reserving the liquid. Leave the onions and the liquid to cool separately.

5 When cool, pack the onions into jars, pushing them down with the handle end of a wooden spoon and 'trapping' the top ones under the 'shoulder' of the jars. This will stop the onions bobbing up above the surface of the liquid. Top up the jars with the cooled pickling liquid. Tap the jars on a folded cloth to release any air bubbles that may be trapped around the sides of the jar.

   Cover the mouth of the jar with greaseproof paper or a cellophane disc, seal with a screw-top lid.

This is a recipe that will need pasteurizing. For full details and illustrations, *see* page 23.

   When the jars are cold, dry, label and store them in a cool dark cupboard until required. Wait at least one month before opening. Keeps for 6 months or more.

Drain and reserve the liquid separately.

Italian pickled asparagus antipasto

Use with cold cuts and cheeses as an antipasto or light lunch. Add to salads, with chopped hard-boiled egg or serve with egg mayonnaise or scrambled egg. To serve, drain and drizzle with extra-virgin olive oil.

Italian pickled asparagus antipasto.

Ingredients

- 1 bunch of local or home-grown asparagus (about 300g)
- 800ml–1ltr of water
- 200ml white wine vinegar
- Pinch of chilli flakes
- 1 teaspoon red peppercorns
- 3 cloves of garlic
- 2 sprigs of thyme
- 2 teaspoons of sea salt

- 1 × 250–350g Kilner or other suitable jar
- Cellophane or greaseproof paper circles and labels

Italian pickled asparagus antipasto ingredients.

Cut each piece of asparagus into three. Blanch in the simmering pickle, then drain.

The drained asparagus should still be crisp.

Top up the jar with the spiced liquid, allowing a 1cm gap at the top.

Italian pickled asparagus antipasto makes the perfect gift.

Before you start

- Wash jar in hot soapy water, rinse, invert and put on a baking tray in a pre-heated oven at 125°C for 20 minutes to sterilize.
- Submerge lid and seal in boiling water for 5 minutes and drain on a clean cloth.

1 Put the water and the vinegar in a large pan. Add the aromatics and salt, bring to the boil slowly.
2 Trim the ends of the asparagus and shave the tougher, lower part of the spears, using a potato peeler.
3 Cut each one into three equal lengths.
4 When the water and vinegar come to the boil, add the cut asparagus and simmer for 3–5 minutes, according to how thick it is. It must remain crisp.
5 After this time drain the asparagus carefully, retaining the spices, herbs and garlic.
6 Fill the prepared jar with the asparagus and aromatics and top up with the cooking liquid, leaving a 1cm gap at the top. Seal the jar and transfer to a clean deep pan. This is a recipe that will need pasteurizing. For full details and illustrations, *see* page 23.

Label and store in the dark. Use after one month.

This pickled asparagus will keep its flavour for 6 months or more.

Variations

Leek and fennel seed

- Cut leeks into 2cm lengths. Use fennel seeds instead of red peppercorns.

Baby sweetcorn and black pepper

- Leave sweetcorn whole and use a teaspoon of black peppercorns instead of red.

Baby pepper antipasto

You can choose to preserve any Mediterranean vegetable this way, according to season, but be careful not to overcook them as they should remain fleshy and retain their colour. If you are unable to source baby peppers, use regular peppers and cut into strips.

Serve, drained, in salads or tarts, as part of an antipasto, sprinkled with freshly chopped herbs and a drizzle of extra-virgin olive oil, with cured meats, cheeses, olives and other Italian treats.

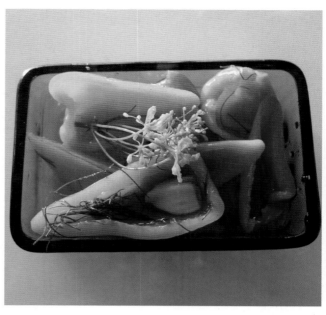

Baby pepper antipasto.

Makes 750g

Ingredients

- 750g mixed colour baby peppers, finger courgettes or baby aubergines
- 12 cloves of garlic, peeled
- 250ml white wine
- 250ml wine vinegar
- 65g white sugar
- 65g coarse salt
- 1 small wine glass extra-virgin olive oil
- 1 teaspoon fennel seeds
- 1 bay leaf
- Plumes of fennel fronds or flowers

- 2 or 3 × 250ml jars or 1 × 500ml jar and lids
- Cellophane or greaseproof paper circles and labels

Before you start

- Wash jars in hot soapy water, rinse, invert and put on a baking tray in a pre-heated oven at 125°C for 20 minutes to sterilize.
- Submerge lids and seals in boiling water for 5 minutes and drain on a clean cloth.

continued overleaf

Bring the ingredients for the pickle slowly to the boil.

1 Put the white wine, wine vinegar, white sugar, coarse salt, 1 small wine glass of extra-virgin olive oil, garlic, 1 teaspoon fennel seeds, 1 bay leaf, in a large pan.
2 Bring slowly to the boil.
3 Cut the baby peppers in half and scrape out the seeds.
4 When the pickle comes to the boil, increase the heat to medium, add the peppers, bring back to the boil, stir in the fresh herbs and switch off.
5 Drain immediately, reserving the liquid.
6 Fill the jars with the warm pepper halves and aromatics, top up with the liquid. Seal the jars, leave to cool.

This is a recipe that will need pasteurizing. For full details and illustrations, *see* page 23.

Label and store in a cool dark place. Use after 1 month and within 3–4 months.

Cut the baby peppers in half and discard the seeds, then add to the pan and bring back to the boil.

Switch off the heat as soon as the fresh herbs have been added.

Drain immediately.

La giardiniera

La giardiniera is a sweet and sour mixed antipasto made in many Italian homes and particularly in Piedmont. There are no hard and fast rules, every cook has their own special recipe and would argue that theirs was best.

You can choose any mixture of vegetables according to the season, but be careful not to overcook them, as they should be crisp and colourful.

Serve cold as a starter or salad or as part of an antipasto.

Makes 1kg

Ingredients

*   750g mixed veg to suit (you can use young courgettes, celery, cauliflower florets, peppers, aubergines, broad beans, borlotti beans, peas or green beans, according to season)
*   250ml white wine
*   250ml wine vinegar
*   65g white sugar
*   65g coarse salt
*   1 small wine glass extra-virgin olive oil
*   1 teaspoon crushed chilli (optional)
*   1 bay leaf
*   1 teaspoon juniper berries
*   12 cloves of garlic
*   Plumes of fennel fronds or flowers
*   Sprigs of fresh oregano or marjoram leaves

*   2 × 500g or 1kg jars and lids
*   Cellophane or greaseproof paper circles and labels

La giardiniera.

Before you start

*   Wash jars in hot soapy water, rinse, invert and put on a baking tray in a pre-heated oven at 125°C for 20 minutes to sterilize.
*   Submerge lids and seals in boiling water for 5 minutes and drain on a clean cloth.

1   Put the white wine, wine vinegar, white sugar, coarse salt, 1 small wine glass of extra-virgin olive oil, 1 teaspoon crushed chilli (if using), 1 bay leaf and 1 teaspoon juniper berries in a large pan. Bring slowly to the boil.
2   Peel and cut the carrots and fennel into strips or cubes. Top and tail and/or pod the beans and peel the onions and garlic

3   When the pickle comes to the boil, increase the heat to medium, add the carrots, celery, onions, beans and garlic. Bring back to the boil. Stir in the fresh herbs and switch off and drain immediately, reserving the liquid.
4   Fill the jars with the vegetables and aromatics, top up with the liquid and seal.

This is a recipe that will need pasteurizing. For full details and illustrations, *see* page 23.

Dry, label and store the jars in a cool, dark place. Use after 1 month and consume within 3–4 months.

CHAPTER 7

Salt of the Earth: Ferments and Pickles

· ·

Pickles and ferments are said to have the potential to protect gut and mind from the frenzy of modern life. In certain parts of the world, such as Eastern Europe, Japan and Korea, fermented pickles are imbedded in mainstream food culture. In the West they have been enjoyed by followers of a more alternative life-style for a while and are rapidly becoming more popular. If your only encounter with fermented vegetables to date has been with a sterile, mass-produced sauerkraut, you may wonder what all the fuss is about: please read on.

WHAT IS FERMENTATION?

Fermentation is the process that uses microbes, bacteria, yeasts and other microorganisms to prepare and preserve foods such as yoghurt, kefir, kombucha and, importantly for us here, vegetables.

Fermented foods are rich in vitamins, minerals and enzymes. As such they are a great tonic and can aid and improve digestion where conventional medication may have failed, re-establishing a healthy gut and intestinal flora, and boosting the immune system. It has long been observed that these preserved foods benefit the digestive tract. Imagine a preserving process that pre-digests food before it even reaches the plate.

What is more, recent research at Stanford University in California discovered that eating fermented foods led to an increase in overall microbial diversity in the gut, with stronger effects from larger servings. Amazingly it also seemed to help prevent inflammation linked to type 2 diabetes, arthritis and stress.

Much has been written on the subject and there are many absorbing books, Dr Caroline Gilmartin's *Fermented Foods: A Practical Guide* (The Crowood Press, 2020) is a good next step if you are keen to learn more.

My purpose here is simply to encourage enthusiasts to add ferments and pickles to their panoply of preservation methods and to show how it is done. Ferments and pickles retain the integrity of the vegetables in them, and involve few ingredients other than a little salt and a few aromatics. They are simple to make, improve our well-being and, best of all, provide an ever-ready vegetable or salad for the busy cook. They can be eaten as they are, added to salads. They can even be stirred through casseroles and stir-fries, but be warned they lose their beneficial effects once cooked.

SALT-ONLY VEGETABLE LACTO-FERMENTATION

Salt was used to preserve foods all over the world before the introduction of refrigeration. Salt pulls the moisture out of food; without moisture, harmful bacteria cannot flourish and only the desired salt-tolerant lactobacilli live and propagate, preserving the vegetables and creating antioxidants, providing a slow fermentation process that is perfect. The salt hardens the pectin in the vegetables, making them crunchy.

◄ Assorted fermented pickles.

Fine sea salt is good for both salting and making brine.

There are two basic ways of preserving vegetables with salt. The first is with a brine solution, such as the Korean kimchi, where vegetables are shredded or cubed to help break down the cell walls and release the sugars to feed the lactobacilli. Whole vegetables such as asparagus, green beans, young carrots, Jerusalem artichokes and gherkins can also be fermented in brine. The other method is by massaging shredded vegetables such as cabbage and runner beans with salt to create their own brine, such as Eastern European krauts, or cut into bite-sized pieces and salted, such as the Japanese shio-zuke.

When vegetables are crushed, they release lactic acid. This then mixes with the salt to create a lactic acid brine, which helps preserve the pickles.

Which vegetable?

Make sure you use young, freshly picked vegetables: organic if you like, but at least home or locally grown when possible.

Cabbages and cucumbers need very little encouragement and start throwing out their juices the moment they are cut into. Just sprinkle them with salt, as the addition of brine is unnecessary.

Whole young vegetables ferment well in brine; older veg are best cubed, sliced or grated. Onions do not contain lactic acid bacteria and therefore are difficult to ferment on their own, but they can be added to other vegetables in a sauerkraut or Kimchi mix. This goes for all onions, spring onions, shallots and leeks. As a rule, add 200g of chopped, shredded or finely sliced onion or leek to every 800g of cabbage. Most other vegetables when fermented in the company of cabbage can be added in a ratio of 60 per cent cabbage.

Heritage varieties of carrots, beets, radish and so on come in a rainbow of enchanting colours and look captivating. Sadly, however, they all take on the deepest, darkest shade very quickly when fermented. This is also true of fermenting red and green cabbages together. The whole pickle turns purple after a couple of days.

Condiments and aromatics

Small amounts of dried mushrooms, seaweed, grated horseradish root and tomato are guaranteed to add umami to the fermenting pot. Finely grated citrus zest can be added to give a pleasant twist in the tail of your ferment. Citrus juice is useful to perk up a dull pickle and when a small amount of top-up of liquid is required. Garlic and root ginger and all other aromatics work well. The choice is yours.

Fish sauce is a traditional seasoning for kimchi. Try adding it to other ferments and experiment with other sauces, such as Worcester sauce, and with mushroom and walnut ketchups. Vegetarians and vegans may prefer to use Henderson's rather than Worcester sauce, which contains anchovy.

Berries and seeds give good bursts of flavour and texture. All ground spices are good to add and in quantity they may add colour to your ferment. Never be afraid of tasting: it is never too late to add extra condiments to spice up a dull pickle.

When adding ground chilli, pimento, chilli flakes and other spicy components, start by adding just a little and then taste. You can always add more.

Always remember that the cooler the ambient and the slower the ferment, the crisper will be the resulting pickle.

A farmers' market is a great place to shop for fresh vegetables. This one is Porta Palazzo in Turin.

Home-fermented vegetables are the ultimate convenience food. Open a jar and serve sprinkled with chopped herbs, seeds and spices (clockwise from top): Cambodian pickled slaw with chili and lime, sauerkraut, kimchi, red cabbage and beetroot kraut with chopped fennel fronds, runner bean kraut; (centre) Jerusalem artichokes with black sesame seeds.

5% brine: standard fermentation brine

Sterilize a jar or jars and leave to cool. Mix 50g of fine sea salt with 1 litre of dechlorinated or filtered water (there is no need to heat the water). Slice or dice some vegetables, layer with the spices of your choice and tamper down, leaving a 2–3cm headspace at the top. Cover with a follower, which can be a whole leaf or a food-grade plastic disc. Then fill the jar with the brine, put a weight on top and leave to ferment for anything from 4 days to 6 weeks. You should notice a few bubbles appearing almost straight away, but the ferment will become livelier after 7 or 8 days.

In the past fermentation brines were stronger, around 10 per cent – in other words, they were saltier. Today we would find such salty brines unpalatable and believe them to be unhealthy. When more salt is used, however, the ferment keeps longer. Vegetables preserved in lighter brines, such as 3–5 per cent, will need to be kept in the fridge once the desired level of fermentation is reached, unless you are fortunate to have a cold pantry, cellar, or some other form of cold storage.

Dechlorinated water

Simply allow the desired quantity of chlorinated water to stand for 24 hours to dechlorinate.

Creating natural leaf and plastic followers.

Followers

A follower can be a whole leaf cut from a vine or a cabbage leaf before it is shredded. It can also be a section of a horseradish leaf or even an oak leaf. I sometimes use a few bay leaves in winter when other leaves are unavailable, but I most often use a disc of white food-grade plastic cut from a lid. The best gizmo for the job is the little plastic disc found in some Italian and Polish pickles, with slots all around them, but to date I have failed to source them to buy.

The idea is that the follower creates a barrier between the air and the top of the ferment where bacteria may be present. Never let the pickled vegetables bob up above the surface of the brine.

Using horseradish, vine or oak leaves has a two-fold benefit in that they also add tannins to the pickle.

Drop lid and weights

The next step is to put pressure on the vegetable to encourage the release of juices from the cell walls and the creation of the salt-tolerant lactobacilli.

You will probably need to improvise. I use a round food-safe plastic disc or lid slightly smaller than the size of the circumference of the jar. This sits on top of the vegetables. If you don't have one just the right size, cut down a lid to fit.

Improvised drop lid and weights. Fill a bottle that will fit the mouth of the jar with water.

Glass and ceramic weights can be sourced on the web.

You will also need a weight to sit on top. Fill with water a smallish jar or bottle that will pass through the neck of the preserving jar or crock. Seal and sterilize the outside before use. Do not use anything that might be corrosive. You could try using a 500ml zip-lock freezer bag filled with water, but make sure it does not leak. At this stage the jar remains open. Once the vegetables are submerged in their own juices, fermentation starts and bubbles appear on the surface of the pickle. The big weight can then be removed and the jars sealed.

You can buy small ceramic and glass weights that fit inside the jar when sealed. The brine slowly rises in the jar, immersing the weight. Leave the jar on its tray, covered with a cloth.

Shop-bought glass weight exerts pressure on the jar-sized plastic follower.

Improvised weight: a jam jar filled with water presses on the ferment below.

Burping

Once you have made your pickle, label the lid with the content and the date, put the jar or jars on a baking tray or in a dish to catch any overflow that might occur as the pickle starts to ferment. Close or seal the jar, but open the jar daily to release any build-up of carbon dioxide. This is called 'burping'. Cover the jar with a clean cloth and leave in a cool corner on the work surface, away from direct sunlight. Leave the pickle to ferment like this for four or five days. You should see visual signs that your pickle is starting to ferment (air bubbles in the jar). After the first four or five days there is no need to continue to burp your ferment.

How long does it take?

A ferment can take between four days and six weeks to develop. When you are starting out, taste regularly. Start tasting after the initial four or five days. Once tasted, you can seal the jar and from then taste only once a week or so for up to six weeks. Some enthusiasts like their pickles mild, some strong. There is no right or wrong way to enjoy them. The longer the ferment, the sharper and more vinegar-like the pickle. Make notes as the flavour develops and refer to them next time. Remember the longer the fermentation period, the more beneficial the ferment, as probiotics are produced through every stage of the fermentation.

Once your pickle tastes the way you like it, transfer the jar to the fridge, which will stop or slow fermentation right down to a minimum.

Other vegetable fermentation

Other fermentation liquids, such as water kafir, whey, kombucha and cider vinegar may be more bio-diverse than brine, but they do not prevent bacteria from flourishing, nor do they inhibit mould growth. What is more, the pickled vegetables are more likely to go soft in these other fermentation liquids and the addition of salt is recommended to crisp up the pickle.

Vegetable fermentation brine

You can also use some of the brine from your previous ferments to bio-boost your brew. Add 50ml for every kilogram of vegetables, along with 50g sea salt and 1 litre of water.

Fermentation vessels and equipment

The School of Artisan Food holds regular and very popular fermenting and pickling courses. Students take home everything they prepare, and recipes have been developed to make smaller portable quantities in 750g or 1kg Kilner-type jars.

Very little equipment is needed when starting out, other than a chopping board, a sharp stainless-steel knife and a suitable jar, but you will need an implement for tamping down the vegetables. Simply use the end of a rolling pin wrapped in foil or a sterile bottle.

One of the advantages of making smaller quantities is variety. Two or three jars can be kept going at a time in the fridge. As one jar empties, start fermenting something new.

If you are self-sufficient, however, and growing most or all of your own produce, you will want to make larger quantities. In that case, simply make bigger quantities and ferment in bigger jars or stoneware crocks of the type known in Germany as a Gärtopf. When making large quantities, it is essential to have a cold cellar, larder or outhouse to work and to store the ferments.

Fermentation classes get through many trays of jars.

Exterior and interior views of a Gärtopf stoneware crock.

Use the end of a rolling pin enveloped in foil or a sterile bottle to tamper down the ferment when bottling.

The jar has integral ceramic weight.

Filling the jar.

Your home ferments provide a ready-made supply of colourful, health-giving vegetables.

When fermenting in bulk, once the pickle has reached the desired state of sour, it can be decanted into smaller, more manageable jars for home consumption, freeing up the fermentation vessel for a new pickle.

Sometimes pieces of garlic or other debris will float proud of the surface and little patches of white and green mould may form on the brine. This is harmless and can be skimmed off and discarded. So long as the pickle looks, smells and tastes good there is no problem.

If your brine goes cloudy, be patient. Once it has fermented it should clear again, but if it does not, simply pour off the brine and replace it with fresh.

Everything and anything you make yourself is beneficial for body and mind. This is doubly so when it comes to ferments and pickles. Fermented food should not be pasteurized (canned) as it is a living, breathing foodstuff and the high temperatures required will stop it fermenting, spoil the texture and dull the flavour.

It is time to get in the kitchen and start experimenting.

Remove any bloom or mould that forms on the surface.

Keeping the crunch in your pickles

The salt-only method hardens the pectin in the vegetables, making them crunchy. Use young, freshly picked veg and work in a cool place: the slower the ferment, the crisper the pickle.

Korean kimchi

With the rise in popularity of Korean food, kimchi has become a global hit. Back in its homeland it is made in every family, according to recipes handed down through the generations: no two family recipes are alike. Vegetables are shredded, brined, spiced and fermented in crocks or jars and then served as side dishes at practically every meal.

In Korea, kimchi is made in autumn, and it is customary at that time of the year for employers to give a kimchi bonus to their workers. The bonus is specifically used to stock up on the necessary ingredients and equipment to make enough kimchi to see a family through the year ahead.

The main ingredients are vegetables and brine made from dechlorinated water and salt, chilli flakes and ground chilli, but you will also need one or two specialist items. These are fish sauce and gochujang, a fermented chilli sauce that is moderately hot and very aromatic. Some mainstream supermarkets stock them, but if you have difficulty finding them try an oriental supermarket or an online store.

Making kimchi together around the kitchen table is a very sociable activity.

Traditionally kimchi is left to ferment in cool cellars, but today the must-have wedding gift of aspirational young Koreans is a kimchi fridge, specially designed to provide the perfect environment for fermentation and storing.

The making and sharing of kimchi in autumn in Korea has been designated a UNESCO Intangible Cultural Heritage of Humanity.

Kimchi can be made with any shredded or cubed vegetable. Chinese leaves or napa cabbage, as it is also known, is generally most associated with the genre. Vegetables are soaked in salty brine for a few hours or overnight. This takes out the bitterness and softens them in both texture and flavour. The cabbage is then drained: spices and an aromatic chilli paste called gochujang, fresh ginger and garlic are mixed through. Rice paste and/or sugar may be added, speeding up the ferment and enriching the texture and flavour. Fish sauce is an optional but truly authentic addition, and squid kimchi is a popular speciality. If you don't eat fish, you can add tamari soy sauce instead.

Traditionally kimchi is made in quantity in large open containers and the head of Chinese leaves is cut into wedges, rather than cut into the bite-sized pieces used in this recipe. The idea of keeping some of the cabbage leaves whole and layering them with the chopped cabbage is to replicate the natural wedges that would be too large to ferment in a jar.

If you want to experiment making kimchi in bulk, use a large open ceramic jar or tub (never use corrosive materials). Proceed as per this recipe, cutting the cabbage into wedges and layering with the other ingredients, leaving the kimchi to ferment open to the air. Be warned it can become unpleasantly smelly, but the flavour remains good.

Kimchi is a great ferment to start with as its hot, spicy, salty flavour is easy to love. Make it hot like it is in Korea, or subtly spicy to suit yourself. Eat it straight away to enjoy the roller coaster of fresh tastes or leave it to ferment to increase the benefits and to create a deeper curve of flavours. It is easy to make, and you can ring the changes, using different vegetables, herbs and spices.

Kimchi ingredients.

Ingredients

- 1 large head Chinese leaves or Napa cabbage, weighing 1kg
- 80g sea salt
- 1 litre cold water (filtered or dechlorinated)
- 200g daikon/mooli radish, carrot or celeriac
- A good handful of chopped kale
- 4 spring onions
- 4 fat cloves of garlic
- 2cm square of ginger
- 1–2 tablespoons chilli flakes, possibly Korean, to taste
- 10–20g ground chilli, paprika or pimento or 1 tablespoon gochujang (fermented chilli paste)
- 10g caster sugar
- 1 tablespoon ground rice
- 2 teaspoons fish sauce or tamari soy (optional)

- 1 × 2-litre or 2 × 1-litre jar

Before you start

- Wash jars in hot soapy water, rinse, drain and put on a baking tray in a pre-heated oven at 125°C for 20 minutes to sterilize. Leave the jars to cool. Alternatively dishwash and use when cooled.
- Submerge lids and seals in boiling water for 5 minutes and drain on a clean cloth.

1 Trim the stalk of the cabbage. Peel off and reserve 3 or 4 of the outer leaves.
2 Chop the rest of the cabbage into bite-sized pieces.
3 Put the reserved leaves and the chopped cabbage in a large bowl.
4 Make the brine by mixing the measured salt and dechlorinated water. Pour over the cabbage and press the cabbage down under the brine.
5 Weight with a plate to keep the leaves below the brine. Cover with a clean cloth and leave overnight or for at least 8 hours.
6 After this time, pour off the brine into a large bowl or jug and reserve for later use.
7 Rinse the cabbage in fresh cold water, drain and squeeze dry.
8 Using a small pan, mix the ground rice with 150ml of cold water. Stir well, using either a wooden spoon or a small whisk, until smooth, set over low heat and simmer until the paste starts to thicken. It should have a pouring consistency. Add a little more water, if necessary, and leave to cool.
9 Chop the garlic finely and grate or chop the ginger. Put it into a large bowl.

Peel off 3 or 4 leaves and chop the rest into bite-sized pieces.

Pour the brine over the cabbage and press down.

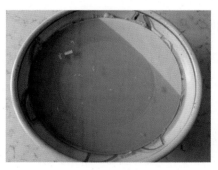

Weight with a plate to keep the cabbage below the surface. Leave overnight.

Pour off the brine and reserve for later.

Rinse the cabbage and squeeze dry.

Slice the spring
onions diagonally.

Add the spring
onions, grated carrot
and cooled ground
rice to the aromatics,
sauces and so on.

Add the chopped
Chinese leaves and
kale. Stir well.

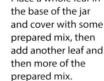

Place a whole leaf in
the base of the jar
and cover with some
prepared mix, then
add another leaf and
then more of the
prepared mix.

10 Finely slice the spring onions diagonally and reserve.

11 Chop the kale and grate the carrot and reserve.

12 Add the spices and sauces to the garlic and ginger and stir well.

13 Add the spring onions, the grated carrot and the cooled ground rice and stir again.

14 Now taste the drained Chinese leaves for saltiness. If it does not taste salty, add 1–2 teaspoons of sea salt to the paste. Kimchi needs salt for flavour. Now add the rinsed and drained, chopped Chinese leaves and the chopped kale and mix well.

15 Pick out the whole Chinese leaves, ready for potting.

16 Take one of the reserved leaves and put it in the base of the jar. You may need to cut it in half. Cover with a few spoons of the prepared mix.

17 Now place another section of leaf on top.

18 Cover with more of the cabbage mix and repeat the process until all the mix has been used, pressing down at every layer.

19 Finish with a whole leaf.

20 Pour a little of the reserved brine into the jar and immerse the kimchi. You will not need much (just enough to soak the cabbage), and leave a headspace of a few centimetres.

21 Seal the jar and set aside to ferment for 3–4 days on a work surface at room temperature. You should see tiny bubbles rising to the surface. Taste to see if it is to your liking. If it is not sour enough, leave for an extra 24 hours and taste again. Either leave the jar open or undo the lid daily to release any pressure that may have built up in the jar.

It is now ready to eat. Store in the fridge, cold cellar or pantry for a month or so.

Cover with more of the cabbage mix and repeat.

Finish with a whole leaf and immerse the kimchi in brine.

Undo the lid daily to release the pressure.

Variations

Cambodian pickled slaw with chilli and lime

- This pickle recipe is based on a popular salad from Cambodia. My immediate response to fermenting it was to create a kimchi, but I could not resist trying it out as a sauerkraut. Both versions were successful – decide which you prefer or try both. Details of the sauerkraut method will be found later in this chapter.

Cambodian pickled slaw with chilli and lime ingredients.

Ingredients

- 1 small white cabbage, weighing 500g (stalk discarded) and leaf finely shredded
- 1 small red cabbage, weighing 500g (stalk discarded) and leaf finely shredded
- 80g sea salt if making a brine (30g salt for sauerkraut)
- 1 litre cold water (filtered or dechlorinated) (no water is needed for the sauerkraut method)
- 2 green (bell) peppers
- 1 shallot
- 6 fat cloves of garlic, finely chopped
- 2 fresh red chillies, finely chopped
- 2 teaspoons chilli flakes
- 1 heaped teaspoon pimento
- 10g palm sugar
- 2 teaspoons fish sauce or tamari soy
- Finely grated zest of 2 limes and juice

- 2 × 750g jars

Before you start

- Wash the jars in warm soapy water, rinse, invert and dry at 125°C for 20 minutes and then leave to cool. Alternatively, dishwash and use when cooled

Kimchi version

1 Trim the stalks of the two cabbages. Peel off and reserve 3 or 4 of the outer leaves and shred the rest of the cabbages.
2 Make the brine by mixing the measured salt and dechlorinated water.
3 Put the reserved leaves and the shredded cabbage in a large bowl and add the brine.
4 Sit another bowl on top.

Add the brine to the reserved leaves and shredded cabbage.

Sit another bowl on top and leave this, weighted down and covered, overnight.

5 Put a weight in the bowl and leave overnight or for 8 hours, covered with a clean cloth. After this time pour off the brine into a large bowl or jug and reserve for later use. Rinse the cabbage in fresh cold water, drain and squeeze dry and return to the bowl.

6 Finely slice the two bell peppers, finely chop the shallot, garlic and chillies, grate the lime zest and juice the limes.

7 Add all this to the cabbage and mix well.

8 Add the spices and the sauce, stir. Now taste the mix for saltiness. If it does not taste salty add 1–2 teaspoons of sea salt to taste. At this stage, if you like it fiery, add more ground chilli to taste.

9 Take one of the reserved leaves and put it in the base of the jar. You may need to cut it in half. Cover with a few spoons of the prepared mix.

10 Now place another leaf on top and cover with more of the cabbage mix. Repeat the process until all the mix has been used.

11 Finish with a whole leaf. Press down well at every layer with the end of a rolling pin or sterile bottle.

12 There should be a headspace of 2–3cm at the top.

13 Pour some of the reserved brine (used for soaking the cabbage) into the jar and fill to the shoulder of the jar. You may not need much. Put a follower on top and a weight on that. For an illustration, *see* the discussion of drop lid and weights on pages 108–109.

Prepare the bell peppers, shallot, garlic, chillies and limes, then add to the cabbage.

Add the spices and the sauce.

Fill the jar with alternating layers of leaves and the cabbage mix until everything has been used.

Leave a headspace of 2–3cm above the whole leaf at the top.

Massage together the shredded cabbage, salt, spices and flavourings.

Before sealing the jar, place a weight on the leaf at the top.

In case the sealed jars overflow, it is better to place them on a baking tray.

Jars should always be left to ferment on a tray, in cool conditions and away from direct light, covered with a clean cloth.

Sauerkraut method only

1 Shred the two cabbages, put in a bowl with 30g of salt and the spices and flavourings.
2 Massage well.
3 Stir in the sliced peppers.
4 Fill the jar, leaving 2cm headspace. Finish with a piece cut from a whole cabbage leaf, then put a weight on top.
5 Seal the jar and put it on a baking tray to catch any overflow.
6 Cover with a cloth and set aside to ferment for 3–4 days on a work surface at room temperature. You should see tiny bubbles rising to the surface. Taste to see if it is to your liking. If it is not sour enough, leave for an extra 24 hours and taste again. Either leave the jar open, or release the lid daily to release any pressure that may have built up in the jar.

It is now ready to eat. Store in the fridge, cold cellar or pantry for a month or so.

Kkakdugi carrot and turnip cubed kimchi (salting)

This punchy, crunchy Korean root-vegetable kimchi, made traditionally with cubes of Japanese daikon or mouli and carrot, is delicious as is, tossed into leaf salads or stirred into casseroles just before serving.

Don't forget that you are in control of the amount of spice you add. In small amounts chilli brings out the flavour of the other ingredients. It does not have to be burning hot.

Daikon is readily available in ethnic greengrocers and is beginning to appear on local market stalls, but it is still slow to go mainstream. If you are unable to source, use young white turnips instead. Gardeners please note, daikon is easy to grow. Like kimchi, kkakdugi is popular in Korean home cooking.

Ingredients

- 350g daikon or turnip (if using daikon, immerse in cold water for 5 minutes to modify the spicy flavour, and then pat dry)
- 350g carrot
- 1 level tablespoon fine sea salt (10g)
- 1 level tablespoon palm sugar (10g)
- 1 finely chopped shallot or 2 spring onions, cut in thin rings
- 2 cloves garlic, finely chopped
- A thumbnail piece of ginger, finely grated
- 20ml fish or tamari soy sauce
- 1 level teaspoon chilli flakes
- 1 level teaspoon gochujang paste

- 1 × 500ml sterile jar and lid

1. Peel and cut the turnip or daikon into 1cm cubes.
2. Peel and cut the carrot into 1cm cubes.
3. Mix the vegetable cubes in a large bowl. Add a level tablespoon of fine sea salt and a level tablespoon of palm sugar, stir, and leave for 30 minutes. Drain off any liquid that has accumulated and reserve.
4. Add the finely chopped garlic, ginger and onion.
5. Now add the fish, or tamari soy sauce, the chilli flakes, gochujang paste and 20ml of the drained liquid. Stir well to distribute the seasonings evenly. Taste and adjust seasoning to your liking. If it is too hot, add more veg; if it is too tame add more chilli.
6. Transfer the kkakdugi to a jar.
7. Press down well.
8. Put a small weight on top.
9. You can eat it straight away, storing it in the refrigerator. Or you can keep it on a kitchen surface to ferment for 3 or 4 days, either open or sealed, until it starts to smell sour. If the jar is sealed, undo the lid daily to disperse the pressure. When it starts fermenting, little bubbles appear on top.

It will keep in the fridge for a month or more.

Finely chop the garlic, ginger and onion.

Transfer the kkakdugi to a Kilner jar.

Hold the kkakdugi down with a small weight.

Leave the jar, either open or sealed, until it starts to smell sour.

Prepared sauerkraut ingredients.

SAUERKRAUT

Master recipe (salting)

Sauerkraut is generally associated with Eastern European countries and particularly with Germany. Like most preserves, homemade is best. Therefore, if you have only tasted mass-produced sauerkraut put any negative preconceptions aside.

Shredding the cabbage and other vegetables, and ultimately massaging them, breaks down the cell walls and encourages the juices from the leaves, submerging them in their own brine.

This recipe can be used to preserve a mixture of any shredded vegetables, such as fennel, kohlrabi, beetroot, celeriac and Jerusalem artichokes, using a ratio of at least 50 per cent cabbage. I have given a variety of flavourings in the ingredients, but you can experiment with other spices, fresh herbs, spring nettles, wild garlic, fresh ginger, fresh turmeric and garlic.

Once salt and aromatics have been added, use your hands to massage the cabbage well to release lactic acid.

Ingredients

- 800g cabbage
- 200g fennel, celery, celeriac or kohlrabi, leek, young nettles or the vegetable of choice
- 20g salt
- 2 teaspoons caraway, cumin seeds or fennel
- You may need some 5% brine to top up the jar (*see* page 107)

- 1-litre jar and lid

Pack the kraut into the jar and press the vegetables down firmly.

Before you start

- Wash jar in hot soapy water, rinse and put on a baking tray in a pre-heated oven at 125°C for 20 minutes to sterilize. Leave the jar to cool. Alternatively dishwash and use when cooled.
- Submerge lid in boiling water for 5 minutes and drain on a clean cloth.

1 Pull off any tough outer leaves and reserve one. Finely shred the tender leaves, cutting out and discarding any tough stalks. Put the shredded cabbage and the other vegetables in a large bowl and mix in the salt and aromatics.
2 Massage for a few minutes. This breaks down the cell walls and releases the lactic acid.
3 The cabbage should now be very wet.
4 Pack the kraut into the jar.

5 Press the vegetables down firmly to get it all in, leaving a 2–3cm headspace at the top of the jar.

6 Cut the reserved leaf down to size to fit the top of the jar.

7 Cover the top of the sauerkraut with the leaf.

8 Put the jar on a tray or dish to catch any overflow, as the kraut ferments.

9 Put a weight on top and leave until the cabbage is completely submerged. Cover with a cloth. Leave on a work surface in a cool place in your kitchen away from direct sunlight. After 24 hours the shredded vegetables should be completely immersed in their own juices. If not, add enough 5% brine to cover the cabbage completely. But first remove the weight. Seal the jar and label the lid.

Cover the sauerkraut with the reserved leaf.

It is important to push the vegetables down under the brine. If the vegetables are left above brine level, white mould will form. If this happens it should be removed straight away.

Fermentation will speed up in warm surroundings or slow down in a cold environment. Once you see small bubbles rising to the surface you will know that fermentation is taking place.

The seal of the jar should be released daily for the first 3 or 4 days to allow the carbon dioxide to escape and prevent a build-up of pressure.

The sauerkraut will be ready to eat after a few days but can be left for up to 6 weeks, by which time the pickle will taste strong and vinegary.

Once the ferment is transferred to the fridge it slows right down.

It will keep in the fridge for a month or more.

Always put your jars of vegetables on a dish or tray to catch any excess liquid that may form and bubble over during fermentation.

Pickled cabbage relish with apple, onion and chopped figs (salting)

Ingredients
- 1kg red cabbage
- 100g red onion, thinly sliced
- 15–20g of sea salt, to taste
- ½ teaspoon of pink peppercorns, crushed
- ½ teaspoon cumin seeds
- ½ teaspoon cinnamon
- 100g apple, diced weight
- 100g dried figs, soaked, dried and chopped
- 50ml whey, apple cider vinegar, Kombucha or left-over pickle juice
- 100ml of dechlorinated water

- 2 × 750ml jars

Before you start
- Wash jars in hot soapy water, rinse and put on a baking tray in a pre-heated oven at 125°C for 20 minutes to sterilize. Leave the jar to cool. Alternatively dishwash and use when cooled.
- Proceed as the above recipe, adding the chopped fruit and the pickle juice, whey, apple cider vinegar or Kombucha directly before packing the kraut into the jars at step 4.

Beetroot, orange and red cabbage sauerkraut ingredients.

Add the orange zest to the cabbage and grated beetroot.

Mix the ingredients thoroughly.

Press down the kraut and leave a headspace of 2–3cm.

Top with a weight and place the jar on a tray in case it overflows.

Beetroot, orange and red cabbage sauerkraut

This kraut is the best. It is gloriously sweet and crunchy, so please try it. It creates just enough juice to keep it fresh. Keep it weighted and keep pushing it down until you transfer it to the fridge. It will not deteriorate.

Ingredients
- 500g red cabbage (shredded weight)
- 165g raw beetroot (grated weight)
- 10g salt
- 3 level teaspoons of caraway seeds
- 3 level teaspoons of mustard seeds
- 1 organic orange

- 1 × 750ml jar

Before you start
- Wash jar in hot soapy water, rinse, drain and put on a baking tray in a pre-heated oven at 125°C for 20 minutes to sterilize. Leave the jar to cool. Alternatively dishwash and use when cooled.

1. Shred the cabbage and put it into a bowl with the spices and salt. Massage well to release the juices from the cell walls.
2. Grate the beetroot and add to the bowl.
3. Finely grate the orange zest, juice the orange and add both to the kraut.
4. Mix thoroughly.
5. Fill the jar, pressing down.
6. Leave a headspace of 2–3cm.
7. Cover with a whole leaf.
8. Top with a weight and sit in a dish or on a tray
9. Carefully follow the directions from step 9 of the Sauerkraut Master recipe on page 120.

Mutters Bohnen: Mother's Sauer-runner beans (salting)

This bean kraut is based on a traditional German recipe made by Frau Schrick in Essen back in the 1950s. In days gone by, large quantities of runner beans, maybe 5kg at a time, were salted away for the winter in huge earthenware jars to see the household through when fresh vegetables became scarce. With no refrigeration, double the amount of salt was needed to preserve the beans, which were stored in a cool dark cellar.

Shredding the beans and then massaging them breaks down the cell walls and encourages the water to leach, submerging the beans in their own juices.

Because runner beans are a prolific crop that all come at once after the rain, they make a natural choice for the fermenting pot. We used to salt beans in Britain too, but in quite a different process. The beans were added little by little, left whole and layered in large quantities of salt, allowing 100g of salt to 500g of beans. More beans and more salt were added until the jars were filled. The beans were rinsed as required and cooked as needed.

Ingredients

- 500g runner beans
- 15g salt
- 1 teaspoon caraway seed

- 1 × 750g Kilner jar

Before you start

- Wash jar in hot soapy water, rinse and put on a baking tray in a pre-heated oven at 125°c for 20 minutes to sterilize. Leave the jar to cool. Alternatively dishwash and use when cooled.
- Boil Kilner seal for 5 minutes.

1 Trim and thinly slice the beans.
2 Put them in a large bowl.
3 Add the salt and the caraway seeds and massage the beans well until the juices start to run.
4 Cover the beans with a plate and put something heavy on top to act as a weight. Let it stand for 24 hours.
5 After this time, the beans will be wet.
6 Fill the jar with the beans, pushing them down with your fist or the end of a rolling pin or bottle as you do so, to encourage the release of the juice. Fill the jar right to the top and keep pressing down to leave a headspace of 2–3cm.

Add salt and caraway seeds to the cut beans and massage.

Cover the beans with a plate and weigh it down for 24 hours.

Press down as you fill the jar to release the juice.

7 Cover the surface of the beans with a food-grade plastic follower.
8 Sit a bottle or a jar filled with water on top to act as a weight. Leave for another 48 hours.
9 After 48 hours, the sliced beans should be completely immersed in their own juices. If not, add enough 3% brine to cover the beans completely.

The beans will be ready to eat after a few days but can be left for up to 6 weeks, as was once the tradition, and then transferred to the fridge.

Trim and scrape the artichokes, and cut into pieces.

Leave to ferment for 3–4 days.

Pickled Jerusalem artichokes (brining)

Also known as sunchokes, the Jerusalem artichokes have a wonderful sweet, earthy taste and a creamy texture, roasted, served in pies and bechamel sauce or made into soup. This delicious tuber, however, has an unfortunate side effect that merits its nickname, the 'fartychoke'.

They grow profusely in the kitchen garden through the winter and are best consumed in small quantity. Fermenting the artichoke, however, expels a lot of the gas before they even reach the plate. A fermented artichoke is a good crunch addition to winter salads.

This method can be used to pickle carrots, fennel and other vegetables.

Ingredients

- 500g of Jerusalem artichokes
- 500ml dechlorinated or filtered water
- 15g fine sea salt
- 1 bay leaf or other fresh herbs

- 1 × 750ml jar

Before you start

- Wash jar in hot soapy water, rinse, drain and put on a baking tray in a pre-heated oven at 125°C for 20 minutes to sterilize. Leave the jar to cool. Alternatively dishwash and use when cooled.

1 Trim and scrape or scrub the artichokes.
2 Cut into 2, 3 or 4 pieces, depending on their size, and fill the jar leaving a headspace of 2–3cm, adding the peppercorns as you do so.
3 Mix the brine and immerse the artichokes. They are solid and should not float to the surface. Add the bay leaf.

  If some do float, you will need a follower to keep them below the surface. As this is a winter crop and the usual leaves are not available, use 3 or 4 bay leaves as in the asparagus recipe below.
4 Leave for 3 or 4 days to ferment. You can eat them at this stage or leave them to ferment longer if preferred.

Pickled asparagus spears (brining)

This is a fun but elegant ferment to make in early summer when asparagus is in season. The weight of a bunch of asparagus varies depending on how fat the spears are, so take this into account. Those used here were thin.

Make sure you choose a tall slim jar, then the asparagus can be preserved whole.

Ingredients

- 2 bunches of asparagus (200g trimmed weight)
- 500ml dechlorinated or filtered water
- 15g fine sea salt
- 1 blood orange
- 1 teaspoon coriander seeds
- 4 bay leaves
- 1 vine leaf or horseradish leaf, when available

- 1 × 750ml jar and lid

Before you start

- Wash jar in hot soapy water, rinse, drain and put on a baking tray in a pre-heated oven at 125°C for 20 minutes to sterilize. Leave the jar to cool. Alternatively dishwash and use when cooled.
- Boil lids for 5 minutes.

1 Stir the salt into the water to make brine.
2 Trim the asparagus, discarding any tough bits.
3 Measure the asparagus up against the height of the jar and trim the base of the spears so that the tips will line up evenly with the shoulder of the jar. Retain any tender pieces you cut off.
4 Fill the jar with the asparagus spears.
5 Finely grate the zest of an orange (I used a blood orange) and crush the coriander seeds.
6 Add the orange zest, the crushed coriander seeds and the offcuts to the asparagus.
7 Make sure the asparagus tips line up with the shoulder of the jar.
8 Add the brine to cover the asparagus tips, that is to the shoulder of the jar. At this stage they bob up above the level of brine.
9 You will now need a follower to keep the asparagus below the surface of the brine. A vine or horseradish leaf is usual, but neither was available, so I used bay leaves.

Pickled asparagus spears ingredients.

Measure the asparagus against the height of the jar.

Finely grate the zest of an orange

Add the offcuts and sprinkle over the orange zest and crushed coriander seeds.

When you add the brine the spears bob above the surface.

10 Trim the pointed ends from the bay leaves and line them to the shape of the lid.

11 Then lay them across the neck of the jar and gently push them down under the brine to ensure all the asparagus stays below the brine level.

Leave for 3 or 4 days to ferment. You can eat them at this stage or leave them to ferment longer.

Bay leaves can be cut and arranged as a follower if nothing else is available.

Gherkins (brining)

Pickling gherkins to perfection takes some trial and much error. This is actually down to the quality and size of the cucumbers. Probably the most difficult aspect of all is the sourcing of small cucumbers as you really do not want them longer than 6 or 8cm; even smaller is better, if possible. I would go as far as to say that home-grown cucumbers are best. Make sure they are freshly picked and do not show any signs of yellowing or wrinkling.

To ferment them successfully you are going to need a stronger salt to water ratio than you need for other vegetables. I have found 10 per cent salt to filtered water is best.

The quantity of brine will vary according to the size of the cucumbers. Any brine you don't use can be refrigerated and used later for another pickle.

Aromatics for gherkins.

Ingredients

- 750g–1kg very small cucumbers, wiped, and stems, flowers or leaves removed
- 750ml of dechlorinated or filtered water (to dechlorinate water, simply run it into a jug or canister the day before you need it and leave to stand for 24 hours)
- 75g fine sea salt
- 2 cloves of garlic, lightly crushed, peeled and cut into slivers
- 1 bay leaf
- 1 dried chilli
- 1 heaped teaspoon coriander seeds
- 1 heaped teaspoon mustard seeds
- 1 heaped teaspoon of fennel seeds
- 1–2 vine or horseradish leaves

- 2 × 500ml jars or 1 × 1-litre jar

Before you start

- Wash jars in hot soapy water, rinse, drain and put on a baking tray in a pre-heated oven at 125°C for 20 minutes to sterilize. Leave the jars to cool. Alternatively dishwash and use when cooled.
- Boil lids for 5 minutes.

1 Measure out the desired quantity of dechlorinated water, add the salt and stir.
2 Put the garlic, bay leaf, chilli, coriander and mustard seeds in the bottom of the jar or jars.
3 Fill the jar with the cucumbers, pushing them down firmly, layering them with the dill or fennel. Do not fill the jar above the shoulder. Fill the jar with the brine. Reserve any remaining brine for topping up the jar as necessary. Make sure the cucumbers are completely covered by the brine.
4 Cover the cucumbers with a follower, preferably vine or horseradish leaves.
5 Check that the follower stays below the surface of the brine.
6 Put the jar on a plate or in a bowl to catch any of the brine that may bubble up. Leave to ferment. Put the lid on loosely. If you put the lid on tightly the jar must be burped daily for the first 3 or 4 days to stop pressure building up. Cover with a cloth and leave on the work surface away from direct sunlight. Check daily and add more brine if necessary.

Divide the aromatics between the jars.

Use vine or horseradish leaves as a follower.

As the contents of the jar ferment, leave the lid on loosely or burp it daily.

In the first instance, the cucumbers will take on a glorious bright green hue, but as they turn sour the colour diminishes to a greyish green and the brine turns cloudy. This is normal. The brine will clear when the cucumbers stop fermenting.

Seal the jar when the cucumbers are to your liking and transfer to the fridge.

Japanese salt-fermented cucumber ingredients.

Western cucumbers need to be peeled, cut in half and deseeded.

Cut the cucumbers into batons, as here, or slices.

Japanese salt-fermented (shio-zuke) cucumber

When vegetables are crushed they release lactic acid. This then mixes with the salt to create a lactic acid brine, which helps to preserve the pickles and add antioxidants. In the past the salt ratio to vegetable was around 10 per cent, but it is possible to make shio-zuke with between 3 and 4 per cent. The process takes 3 or 4 days.

Use this recipe to cure any vegetable or mix of vegetables. If insufficient lactic acid is created to engulf your pickle, top up the jar with a little 3% brine, using 15g of sea salt to 500ml filtered or dechlorinated water.

Ingredients

- 1kg cucumbers (3), cabbage, aubergine, carrot, turnip, daikon, fennel etc.
- 30g salt
- Personalize your pickle by adding either a small piece of yuzu (Japanese citrus) or citrus zest, chilli, ginger, garlic or kombu (seaweed) to the jar
- Tamari soy sauce for serving

- 500g jar with lid or a Kilner jar

Before you start

- Wash jar in hot soapy water, rinse and put on a baking tray in a pre-heated oven at 125°C for 20 minutes to sterilize. Leave the jar to cool. Alternatively dishwash and use when cooled.
- Boil lid or seal for 5 minutes

1. If using Western cucumbers, you will need to peel, cut them in half lengthways and deseed them.
2. Then cut into pieces, either slices or batons.
3. Put them in a large bowl and sprinkle with half the salt and massage gently. Water will start leaching immediately.
4. Layer the cucumber pieces in the jar with the remaining salt.

5 Personalize your shio-zuke by adding a piece of root ginger, kombu or similar.

6 Push them right down with a rolling pin wrapped in foil so that the jar is crammed full.

7 The level of the lactic acid brine should already nearly engulf the cucumber.

8 Lay an appropriately sized round plastic disc on top and put a small weight on top of this.

9 Stand the jar in a bowl or on a tray. Keep in a cool place on the work surface, away from direct sunlight. Cover with a cloth but keep an eye on it. The jar will start filling up and brimming over almost at once. As the water leaches out, push the disc down. As the level drops, add in a few more pieces of cucumber, if you have any to spare.

10 After 24 hours the cucumber should be immersed in its own juices. At this point you can remove the weight and leave the jar open or seal the jar, but remember to open the jar to release the pressure in the jar daily. Leave to ferment for another 3 days, then transfer to the fridge with the lid on. The shio-zuke will have darkened slightly.

When ready to serve, take out what you need, seal the jar and return to the fridge.

Note that a white bloom may form on the brine, but do not worry about this as it will wash off.

Rinse the shio-zuke under running water, squeeze out excess water and lay on kitchen paper to dry. Then serve with one or two drops of light soy.

Use within a month stored in the fridge.

Add a piece of root ginger to be different.

Be aware that the jar will start filling up and brimming over almost at once.

Mixed Japanese su-zuki

Rice vinegar pickle, or su-zuki as it is called in Japanese, is a popular and very simple pickle media. The pickles have a subtle balance of sweetness and acidity, and the initial light salting helps retain the integrity of the vegetables.

This is delicious added to salads, served as a sashimi garnish, chopped through vinegared rice or as a side dish with oriental dishes.

Once vinegar is added to a pickle it is no longer strictly a ferment, but I hope you will forgive me for including it here, as it's worth it.

Ingredients

- 1 large carrot or turnip
- ½ cucumber
- 6 spring onions cut in diagonal Julienne
- 2% of the weight of the vegetables of salt
- 1 slice of ginger root
- 1 dried chilli
- 200ml rice vinegar
- 100ml mirin

- Variations: daikon, aubergine, spring onions, baby carrots, asparagus, small courgettes, broad beans and green beans, samphire grass (use just a teaspoon of salt, as samphire is already salty)
- For these prepare in the same way, but cut the ginger root into paper thin slices

- 1 × 500ml jar

Before you start

- Wash jar in hot soapy water, rinse and put on a baking tray in a pre-heated oven at 125°C for 20 minutes to sterilize. Leave the jar to cool. Alternatively dishwash and use when cooled.
- The lid should be boiled for 5 minutes and then drained.

1 Peel the carrot or turnip and cut in diagonal batons.
2 Peel, deseed and cut the cucumber into diagonal batons.
3 Clean the spring onions.
4 Slice the spring onions diagonally.
5 Put in a bowl and sprinkle with the salt and massage gently. The water will start leaching immediately.

Cut the carrot in diagonal batons.

Slice the spring onions diagonally.

Massage the carrots, spring onions and salt together.

6   Weight and cover with a cloth and leave for 24 hours.
7   At this point remove the weight, drain off the liquid and rinse the vegetables.
8   Pat dry on a clean cloth.
9   Pack the vegetables into the sterile jar.
10 Fill the jar with a mixture of two parts rice vinegar and one part mirin.
11 Add a slice of ginger root and a piece of chilli.
12 Seal the jar and store for a week before using. Keeps for 3 months.

Pat the rinsed vegetables dry on a clean cloth.

Top up with a mix of rice vinegar and mirin, and add the ginger root and chilli.

The su-zuki should be ready to eat after a week.

You may use pumpkin, butternut or any other squash.

Add salt to the pumpkin slices or cubes and massage well.

Add the chopped spices and garlic.

If necessary, take out the weight and top up with 3 per cent brine.

Spiced pumpkin

This is a useful and refreshing variation on a theme. Add it to salads, serve it as an accompaniment or a condiment with toasted pumpkin seeds. You could even try adding it to stir-fries just before serving.

Ring the changes by trying butternut squash, sweet potato or sliced courgettes.

Ingredients

- 600g pumpkin and other squashes (peeled and deseeded), or sweet potatoes
- 15g fine sea salt
- 3 cloves of garlic, finely chopped
- 1 teaspoon ginger root, finely grated
- 1 teaspoon coriander seeds, crushed
- 1 teaspoon cumin seeds, crushed
- 1 teaspoon ground cinnamon
- 1 teaspoon chilli flakes
- Finely grated zest of lemon
- Extra 3% brine to top up as necessary

- 1 × 750ml or 2 × 350ml jars

Before you start

- Wash jars in hot soapy water, rinse and put on a baking tray in a pre-heated oven at 125°C for 20 minutes to sterilize. Leave the jars to cool. Alternatively dishwash and use when cooled.

1 Peel the pumpkin, cut into wedges, discard the seeds and scrape away the hairy insides.
2 Slice or cube the pumpkin into bite-sized pieces.
3 Put in a bowl, add the salt and massage well for about 5 minutes or until the vegetable starts to leach its juices.
4 Add the finely chopped garlic and the spices and massage again. Cover with a plate and leave for 30 minutes, then massage again. Add the lemon zest and lemon juice.
5 Fill the jars and place a follower and a weight on top. Leave to stand until the vegetables are engulfed in their own juices. Cover with a cloth. Leave on a tray (to catch any liquid that may bubble over as the pickle ferments) in a cool place in your kitchen away from direct sunlight.
6 After 24 hours the chopped vegetables should be completely immersed in their own juices. If not, take out the weight and top up the jar with 3% brine

(15g of fine sea salt to 500ml filtered/dechlorinated water). Seal the jar, label and date. Leave the jar on a tray on the work surface, covered with a clean cloth, for 3 days. Open the jar every day to release any trapped gases.

The pickle can be left to ferment for anything from a week to 6 weeks. When starting out it is a good idea to keep tasting, say once a week, until you find the level of sour that suits you.

After this time, store in the fridge where it will keep for at least 2 or 3 months.

KOMBUCHA: TEA-FIZZ

To make fermented tea you are going to need a 'mother' scoby, a symbiotic culture of bacteria and yeast, which can be obtained from www.happykombucha.co.uk. It comes in a vacuum pack along with 125ml of kombucha, which is essential to make your first brew. Once you have made your first brew, you can divide the scoby and give half to a friend or make a double batch. The important thing, as with vinegar and sourdough mothers, is to keep feeding it, to keep it going. The scoby comes with full instructions and explanations.

Ingredients
- 2 litres of filtered or dechlorinated water
- 175g white sugar
- 3–6 good-quality teabags or 3–4 heaped teaspoons of loose-leaf black or green tea
- 1 scoby and 125ml unflavoured kombucha (available from www.happykombucha.co.uk)

Equipment
- 2.5-litre Kilner jar or similar and 4 × 750ml jars, washed in soapy water, rinsed, drained and heated at 125°C for 20 minutes
- A tea ball, if using loose leaf tea
- A large teapot or brewing vessel
- A piece of muslin, large enough to fold double over your brewing jar

The method is simple. Boil the water. Add the teabags or loose-leaf tea enclosed in a tea ball to the pot or brewing vessel, this should be made of stainless steel, earthenware or Pyrex. Add the water and leave to brew to your taste. Add the sugar, stir, strain and leave to cool. On no account should the scoby be added when the tea is still hot.

When cold, transfer the tea to a 2.5-litre brewing jar. Carefully add the scoby – light side up, straggly, yeasty bits hanging down – together with the kombucha. Cover with a piece of muslin, folded double. Secure with an elastic band and leave between 7 and 30 days to sour.

Do not leave in direct sunlight. Cover with a clean cloth and leave on a kitchen worktop.

Taste every few days to see how the flavour changes over time and how you like it best.

When it is to your taste, divide between 4 × 750ml jars; put the scoby back in the brewing jar with 200ml of the freshly made kombucha ready to start again. Store at room temperature, not in the fridge. Do not overfill the jars. You will need room to add the fruit, herbs or flowers, plus 2cm headroom. Seal and refrigerate.

Flavouring your tea-fizz: secondary fermentation

You should now have 3 × 500ml of kombucha plus an extra jar for topping up.

For each of the three jars, you will need:

- 200–300g of raspberries, strawberries, cherries, blueberries or blackberries, lightly crushed

or

- the peeled zests of 2 citrus fruits (lemon, orange or lime)

or

- 1 quail egg-sized piece of ginger and 1 stick of lemongrass, crushed

Open the jars, add either the crushed fruit of choice, the citrus zest or the crushed ginger and lemongrass to each one. Top up each jar but do not overfill, leave a 2cm gap at the top and seal the jars. Make sure you leave at least 200ml of unflavoured kombucha with the scoby to make the next batch.

Cover with a cloth and keep on a work surface away from direct sunlight.

Leave for 2–3 days, strain into bottles and refrigerate.

Keeps a month or more, but the flavour diminishes over time.

Do not on any account use the flavoured kombucha to store the scoby or make a new batch of kombucha.

CHAPTER 8

Gone to Pot:
Pots, Confits, Rillettes and Rillons

· ·

Today we have refrigerators and freezers and there is no need to pot foods to preserve them, but potting creates intense and delicious new flavours and melt-in-the mouth textures. Burying meat and fish in fat not only preserves it, but enriches and softens it, adding a new luxuriance.

HOW TO POT

There are four distinct forms of potting. The first is the French version, the rillons, rillettes and confits, which are slow cooked in fat, tenderizing the legs of game birds and tougher cuts of meat. Then there is British potting, the encapsulation of the likes of tiny shrimp, scraps of succulent lobster, creamy dark crab meat and flaky haddock in cushions of clarified butter. Third, the vintage leftover classic, potted meat and fish, where minced leavings are creamed with the last vestiges of sauces, gravy and cream, spiced, potted, cooked in a bain-marie and submerged under a veil of clarified butter. Lastly there is the wonder of potting in olive oil to preserve rabbit, tuna and chicken.

◀ Potted venison and confit of duck, served with toasted brioche and redcurrant, or crab apple jelly, make delicious picnic, light lunch or starter fare.

A potted history

The howling desert miles around,
The tinkling brook the only sound –
Wearied with all his toils and feats,
The traveller dines on potted meats;
On potted meats and princely wines,
Not wisely but too well he dines.

R.L. STEVENSON

Pots and pies were the first convenience foods. Cooked meats, poultry, game and fish could be rendered both portable and long keeping by being processed in some way (probably with some saltpetre as well as sea salt), potted and then covered by a thick layer of melted suet, pork, duck

Fifty/Fifty

Traditionally potting was carried out in 100 per cent fat, which was essential to preserve meat in the days before refrigeration. To our twenty-first-century, health-conscious minds, however, all that fat could seem scary. I have therefore developed a method using 50 per cent fat and 50 per cent stock, which ensures a lighter product but does not diminish the eating experience. The fat rises to the top, encapsulating and enriching the meat or fish and softening it. The stock-created juices in the bottom half of the jar turn to jelly, making a lighter but an equally delicious medium for potting.

or goose fat and clarified butter. Or it could be enveloped in an inedible paste and slow cooked overnight in a bread oven and left there until cold and set hard The food inside was thoroughly cooked, destroying any bacteria, and then protected from airborne bacteria by the paste or the fat. This was an efficient way of preserving cooked foods long before refrigeration came along. It was the precursor of the modern vac-pack, not vacuum sealed in plastic but rather sealed under a covering of fat or enclosed in a paste made with flour and water. Recipes often suggested using either pots or paste cases, or in some cases both.

Spices were added to the pot, not only for their flavour but for their antimicrobial and antiseptic properties. Common aromatics that we still associate with preserves and pickles, especially cloves, ginger, black pepper, anise, cinnamon, allspice, mace, nutmeg and black pepper, helped not only flavour the food but preserve it. Garlic and onions, which are also antibacterial, were added to enhance flavour and further protect and conserve.

The fat was topped with black pepper and dried herbs to ward off flies.

In her book *Food in England* (Macdonald, 1954) Dorothy Hartley ascribes the development of potting and drying to early sea voyages, and cites Hannah Woolley's recipe from *The Compleat Servant-Maid* (1691) for what she refers to as 'shipload storage' or 'poultry for export':

Take a good company of Duck or Mallards, pull them, and draw them, and lay them in a Tub, with a little Pepper and Salt for twenty four hours, then Truss and Roast them, and when they are roasted let them drain from their Gravy, for that will make them corrupt, and then put them handsomely into a pot, and take the fat which came from them in the Roasting and good store of Butter [this would be salt butter], and melt them together in a Pot set in a Kettle of boyling Water [a bain-marie], put therein good store of Cloves bruised a little, some sliced Mace, Nutmeg, Bay-leaves and Salt, and let them stew in the Butter a while, and then while it is hot pour it over your Fowls in the Pot, and let the Pot be filled, so that the Fowls be covered, then lay a Trencher upon them, and keep them down with a weight or stone untill they be cold, then take of the same kind of Spice which you did put into your Butter, beat it very fine and strew over it, and lay some Bay-leaves on the top, so cover it up, they will keep a good while.

WHICH FAT?

Use any kind of natural fat. I do not recommend spreads or substitute fats as they do not set hard in the way that natural fat does. Choose the fat that most marries with what you are potting. When potting goose, pork and duck there should be enough fat around the flesh to complete the potting process. It is worth noting that you should always have to hand some extra duck and goose fat (readily available in jars from supermarket and butchers). Rendered pork fat is not generally available, so buy some pork back fat or something else the butcher recommends and melt it down yourself.

Game birds and meat carry little fat. Therefore use goose or duck fat with game birds, and use beef dripping with venison and pork fat with wild boar. It is not the end of the world if you run out of one fat – just use one of the others.

For fish, seafood and leftovers use butter, but it must be clarified as the milk solids in the butter do not keep.

Rendering your own fats
Duck fat and goose fat are readily available in jars, but you may like to render your own pork fat as it is always useful to have some back-up fat to top up with.

While on the subject, pour off and collect the fat that drains from meat when cooking, before making sauces and gravy with the pan juices. It is useful for all sorts of culinary purposes.

Are saturated fats bad?
Our grandmothers and great-grandmothers always kept a dripping pot to hand, at least until butter and natural fats started to receive bad press. There is, however, a growing body of research showing that the low-fat diet trend dating from the 1960s was misguided. A study published in 2016 concluded that consuming butter is not linked to a higher risk of heart disease and might even be slightly protective against type 2 diabetes. This goes against the longstanding advice to avoid butter because it contains saturated fat. What is more, it says that cutting back on fat, even the saturated kind, is doing more harm than good.

The author of the report, Dr Dariush Mozaffarian, Dean of the Friedman School of Nutrition Science and Policy at Tufts University in Boston, has a very down to earth approach: 'In my mind, saturated fat is kind of neutral overall … Vegetable oils and fruits and nuts are healthier than butter, but on the other hand, low-fat turkey meat or a bagel or cornflakes or soda is worse for you than butter.'

Sourcing ingredients

The best source of meat or fish is always going to be your local butcher and fishmonger if you are lucky enough to have them. On the borders of Herefordshire, Gloucestershire and Wales we are fortunate to still have both. Game varieties come and go in and out of season quickly and can easily be missed unless you are a regular visitor to such shops.

For me the appearance of seasonal game birds and waterfowl in late summer is a pure moment of culinary joy. They are an inspiration for seasonal ingredients, seasonal recipes and seasonal eating.

The arrival of Wye and Severn salmon at the fishmonger in June used to create a similar thrill. That was when local salmon were two a penny and 'salmon teas' were proudly proclaimed on sandwich boards outside hotels, cafes and restaurants in the vicinity of the great salmon rivers. Today there are emergency byelaws in place to protect dwindling stocks and fish caught must be returned to the river. Let us hope it is not too late for what was once a local industry.

Potted duck canapes enriched with marmalade and orange zest, and potted venison crowned with juicy pomegranate jewels.

How to serve

The French classics are rich and make lavish starters and luscious picnic fayre that can be served in many ways. Stir warm rillons, rillettes and confits through a crisp leaf salad and serve with crusty bread for a light lunch. Reheat the rillons, drain off the fat into a frying pan and sauté potato or cabbage and serve with the meat.

Serve confits of rabbit with chilli-apple jelly, guinea fowl with crab apple jelly, pheasant with redcurrant jelly or duck with marmalade on toasted brioche. Potted slow-cooked venison and wild boar rillettes eat well with Italian crostini or bruschetta and rose petal or redcurrant jelly. They also make delicious pie fillings (for recipes *see* Chapter 3).

Serve creamy potted meat and fish, potted crab and shrimp with Melba toast, toasted rye bread, good old-fashioned wholemeal toast or in a sandwich.

Equipment

When salting, make sure you use shallow, non-corrosive dishes: stainless steel, plastics and ceramics are all good.

When needing to weigh down the meat during salting, find a plate or non-corrosive dish that fits neatly inside the salting vessel and over the meat in order to press it down and encourage the liquid to leach out. A storage jar or bottle can be put on the plate to create extra weight.

Slow cookers, earthenware and Le Creuset-type cast-iron casseroles are all good to use for the next stage of slow cooking.

Kilner jars are the perfect potting vessel as the lids are attached and they have a rubber gasket that seals them fast. They also look good on the table. Use smaller pots unless you know you are going to use it all up quickly. Use 300g, 400g or 500g for larger amounts, 150g, 200g or 250g pots for small amounts and gifts.

Sterilization

Sterilization is an essential part of preserving as it destroys the harmful bacteria, yeast or fungi that linger on the jars and could make your preserves go bad. In other words, it helps protect the end product.

All equipment should be washed, using hot soapy water. It is only the jars and lids that need to be sterilized.

Wash jars and lids in hot soapy water and then rinse them. Invert the clean jars on a baking tray and put in a hot oven at 125°C for 20 minutes.

Putting jars and lids through the dishwasher will also sterilize, but please don't use a full dishwasher cycle to sterilize a few jars.

The rubber gaskets, like jar lids, need boiling for 4 minutes, submerged in water.

CONFITS, RILLONS AND RILLETTES

These are the French classics of the potting genre, made with duck, guinea fowl, rabbit, pheasant and other game.

Confits are most associated with confits de canard (duck) and game bird legs, but there is no reason not to make confits of chicken should you wish. I have included a recipe for the traditional confits de canard with variations for guinea fowl, rabbit and pheasant. All the recipes can be interchanged.

Where confits are traditionally made with the whole legs, rillons are the natural sections that the legs fall into when slow cooked and pulled off the bones. Rillettes are created by shredding the flesh with two forks. The flesh can be further processed by pounding and sieving, or put through a food processor to create a smooth pâté-like consistency.

How it works

The legs of duck and game birds (or indeed the whole bird) are salted and weighted for several hours. The liquid that leaches out is discarded and the flesh wiped dry. Bacteria cannot flourish when deprived of water.

The meat is wiped down, fat, stock and antiseptic aromatics are added and the whole is slow cooked, thus destroying any lingering bacteria.

The meat is taken off the bone, separated into pieces and transferred to a sterile pot where it is engulfed in its own pan juices.

The pot is closed and tapped on a folded cloth to disperse any bubbles that may have collected between the meat pieces. After this the level of the juices may fall and you may need to top up the jar with more juices, if available; melt some more fat if necessary.

As the confit cools and sets, the juices turn to jelly in the bottom of the jar and the fat rises to the top. All the meat must be pushed under the top layer of fat. If any bits poke out above the fat once it has set solid, more fat should be added to completely seal the meat inside. The jar can then be sealed.

Rillons, rillettes and smooth pastes should all be completely sealed under a layer of fat before the jar is finally closed and stored in the fridge.

It will keep in the fridge for a month or more, if you can resist it for that long.

How safe is it?

If we buy a product that has been vacuum packed, it is stamped with a sell-by or use-by date. We are completely relaxed about following it. If we discover it smells bad or has gone mouldy when we open it, we would take it back to where we bought it or throw it away. The packaging may have been accidentally punctured or the product may have been contaminated before being sealed.

When we make our own, we do not have the luxury of a sell-by date, but we have our sense of smell, our sense of taste and our common sense to rely on. I recommend keeping home-potted luxuries for a month. When testing recipes, however, I have kept pots in the fridge for up to six months and they were still fine: all that happened was that they had lost some of their flavour, so there's no point in keeping them for that long. If you take a potted item out of the fridge and it has an unpleasant odour, just throw it away. If you have kept an item longer than you intended, then smell it. If it smells good, taste a tiny bit and if it tastes good, eat it.

Use potted food up quickly once opened. If you don't use it all, level the contents of the jar that are left and pour a little melted fat over the top to reseal. This will ensure freshness a little longer.

Serve the confit reheated, stirred through salad with crusty bread or spread on toasted brioche or crostini style with homemade apple, crab apple, gooseberry or currant jelly. Confit of duck is also good with marmalade.

Confits de canard (potted duck)

This versatile slow-cooked recipe is easy to prepare, can be made ahead of time and is delicious. Serve as a starter or as finger food. Strip the meat from the bone, pot and serve on toasted brioche with dabs of jelly. It will keep for a month or more in the fridge, providing instant luxurious fodder for parties and picnics.

When serving as a main course, cut the leg bones off at the knuckle. Duck legs are relatively inexpensive and confit's most fitting partner is the humble mashed potato. Make a fresh green salad and your winter feast is complete. I generally make four: pot two and then eat two.

Makes 2 × 500g or 4 × 250g Kilner jars, or serves 4 as a main course

Ingredients

- 4 duck legs
- 1 level tablespoon coarse sea salt
- 4 thyme sprigs
- 1 bay leaf
- 2 garlic cloves, crushed
- Juice and zest of 1 orange
- 1 teaspoon freshly ground black pepper
- ½ teaspoon ground cinnamon
- 100ml good stock
- 100g rendered pork, duck or goose fat
- A crumpled sheet of greaseproof or baking parchment
- Extra fat to seal

Before you start

- Wash Kilner jars and jars with lids (if using) in hot soapy water, rinse, invert and put on a baking tray in a pre-heated oven at 125°c for 20 minutes to sterilize.
- The rubber gaskets, like lids, need boiling for 5 minutes, submerged in water.

1 In advance, put the legs in a single layer in a shallow dish, sprinkle with the salt.

2 Use a plate as a weight, or you could even put a storage jar or something else heavy on top. Leave overnight in a cool place.

3 The following day pour off the leached liquid and discard. Wipe the legs with a paper towel and put in an ovenproof dish with a lid. Arrange the legs, preferably in a single layer, sprinkle all the dry ingredients over them and add the liquids. Pour the stock around the legs and spoon the fat over them.

continued overleaf

Put the legs in a shallow dish and sprinkle with salt.

Weight them down with a plate and leave overnight.

Arrange the legs in an ovenproof dish. Add the other ingredients and pour in the stock.

With the crumpled baking parchment in place, cover with the lid and cook overnight.

When the meat is ready the flesh will fall off the bones.

Pull the flesh off the bones with two forks.

Fill the jar and place a strip of the orange peel on top of the meat.

The other legs can be shredded in the same way or served with mashed potato and a salad.

4 Crumple a sheet of baking parchment and run it under the cold tap, shake and use it to fill the space above the legs.

5 Cover the dish with the lid and cook in a very low oven at 80–100°C/Gas Mark ¼ or in a slow cooker for 8 hours or overnight.

6 When the legs are ready the flesh will literally fall off the bone.

7 Put one of the legs on a plate.

8 Using 2 forks, pull the flesh off the bones, discarding the fat and skin, unless liked.

9 Transfer the meat to a sterile jar.

10 Now strip the meat from the second leg and fill the jar.

11 Press down gently and top with a strip of the orange peel.

12 Either strip the meat from the other legs to pot or serve them whole with mashed potato and a salad.

13 Pour off half the pan juices and fat.

14 Top up the jar with the juices to immerse the meat.

15 Close the jar and tap on a folded cloth to ensure there are no bubbles, gaps or air pockets between the pieces of meat. If some remain, poke a sterile skewer or a fine knife blade down the side of the jar to disperse them.

16 If any bits of meat stick up above the fat, press them down under the juices with a small spoon. If the level of the juices has fallen, add extra juices to top up.

17 Leave overnight in the fridge to set. In the morning check the level of the meat and the juices. You will probably find the meat is now proud of the juice. In this case add more juices, if available. Otherwise melt a little extra duck or goose fat to complete the seal.

18 Seal the jar. Note that when the pot cools the fat rises to the top of the jar, while the juices sink to the bottom creating a delicious solid jelly.

This will keep in the fridge for a month. Use within a few days once open.

To serve as a smooth pâté, process the meat with enough juices and/or stock to make a smooth thick paste, add two tablespoons of duck fat and blend well. Transfer the paste to the jar and cover with a thick layer of fat.

Pour off half the pan juices and fat, then top up the jar.

Release any trapped air with a skewer or knife.

If any of the meat is proud of the juice once set, add some more juices or fat.

As the jar cools the fat rises to the top and the juices sink to the bottom.

Guinea fowl, lemon, herbs and white wine

- Confits, whether guinea fowl, duck, chicken or pheasant, are delicious served on the bone, as a main course with mashed potato and a salad.

Ingredients

- 4 guinea fowl or chicken legs
- 1 dessertspoon of coarse sea salt
- 4 sprigs of rosemary
- 4 large sage leaves
- 2 garlic cloves, crushed
- Juice and finely grated zest of 1 lemon
- 1 teaspoon freshly ground black pepper
- 100ml good stock or miso
- 100ml Verdicchio or other good Italian dry white wine (Note: add with the stock and fat if used)
- 100g rendered pork, duck or goose fat

Use the method for confits of duck.

Guinea fowl, lemon, herbs, and white wine makes a delicious meal served with mashed potato and a salad.

Rabbit, gin, juniper berries and rosemary

Ingredients

- 1 whole rabbit, cut into portions
- 1 level tablespoon of coarse sea salt
- 4 large sprigs of rosemary
- 8 juniper berries
- 4 garlic cloves, crushed
- 1 teaspoon freshly ground black pepper
- 100ml good stock or miso
- 100ml Orvieto or other good Italian dry white wine (Note: add with the stock and fat if used)
- 100g rendered pork, duck or goose fat

Use the method for confits of duck.

Pheasant, port wine and pomegranate molasses

Ingredients

- 4 pheasant legs
- 1 dessertspoon of coarse sea salt
- 4 large sage leaves
- 2 bay leaves
- 2 garlic cloves, crushed
- 1 teaspoon freshly ground black pepper
- 100ml good stock or miso
- 100ml tawny port wine (Note: add with the stock and fat if used)
- 100g rendered duck or goose fat

Use the method for confits of duck.

Rillettes and rillons of pork

Pork rillons and rillettes are a wonderfully warming, aromatic, winter treat. Rillettes are traditionally made with lumps of belly pork cooked slowly, carefully shredded with forks and then potted in a deep layer of pork fat to preserve. Rillons are the solid little cubes of meat before they are shredded and can be served hot or cold with a salad, in a tart, or with pickles. Try gently re-heating the rillons (make sure you undo the wire clip before reheating in the oven, otherwise the glass will crack), pouring off the fat and using it to fry either sliced potato or shredded cabbage, then serve with the meat. The recipe here should serve four.

When buying belly pork, the cook will generally look for a piece that is as lean as possible, but to make good rillettes and rillons of pork you need the belly pork to be surrounded in fat.

Ingredients

- 500g fat belly pork, rind removed
- 1 teaspoon coarse salt
- 2 sprigs of fresh rosemary
- ½ teaspoon ground nutmeg

- 1 × 500ml or 2 × 250ml preserving jars

Before you start

- Wash Kilner jars and jars with lids (if using) in hot soapy water, rinse, invert and put on a baking tray in a pre-heated oven at 125°C for 20 minutes to sterilize.
- The rubber gaskets, like lids, need boiling for 4 minutes, submerged in water.

Pork rillons served with fried potatoes and salad.

The Rillons, Rillettes and Confit Code

- Joint or cut the meat into pieces
- Salt or marinade overnight
- Slow cook at between 80°C and 120°C for 6 hours
- Drain off fat and juices
- Take poultry and game meat off the bone
- For rillettes, reduce to a rough paste or shred with a fork, add melted fat and pan juices
- Pack into sterile pots
- Cover with a layer of fat
- Seal the jar and store in the refrigerator

Pork rillons and rillettes ingredients.

Add a little water, followed by the salt, rosemary and nutmeg.

When cooked, strain the pork pieces and reserve the juices.

For rillons, pack the pork pieces into a jar and pour the juices over the top.

To make rillettes, shred the pork before packing it into the jar.

Seal the top with a layer of pork fat.

1 Cut the belly pork into neat pieces about 2–3cm square and put in a slow cooker or casserole dish with a lid.

2 Add enough water to cover the base of the casserole dish, say 150ml. Add the salt, rosemary and nutmeg.

3 Crumple a sheet of baking parchment and run it under the cold tap, shake and use it to fill the space above the pork.

4 Put the lid on and cook overnight, at your oven's lowest setting (80–110°C) or in a slow cooker.

5 Strain the pork pieces.

6 Reserve the pan juices.

7 For rillons, pack the pork pieces into a sterile preserving jar and level.

8 Pour the pork juices over the top to seal, ensuring that the pork is buried completely under the fat and juice.

9 Close the jar and tap on a folded tea towel to disperse any air bubbles.

10 To make rillettes the pork should be shredded carefully with forks and mixed with pork fat and then packed into jars.

11 Seal the top with a layer of pork fat. Check that there are no pieces of pork sticking up above the fat. Top up with more fat if necessary and seal the jar.

Rendering pork fat

- Back fat, as the name implies comes from the back of the pig.
- When rendered, by melting at a low temperature to make lard, it is perfect for frying and making rillons, rillettes and confits with lean meats, such as game.
- Ask your butcher for 500g or more of pork back fat.
- Put it in a roasting tin in a pre-heated oven at 120°C and leave until the fat has melted. This should take about an hour.
- Strain the fat and transfer it to a storage jar.
- Keep in the fridge and use as needed.

Rendering pork fat.

COUNTRY HOUSE POTTING: GAME AND WILDMEAT

This is the traditional British way to pot game and wild meat. Venison comes in and out of season through the year depending on species, which means you should be able to source it for the table throughout the year. Game birds and mallards are in season from either August, September or October, providing a whole new and exciting field of eating for the colder months ahead. Wild boar, Muntjac, rabbit and pigeon have no closed season and are fair game all year long. Like other preserving disciplines, potting captures the season's plenty to enjoy at leisure. The portability of potted fayre meant that, before refrigeration was invented, game could be easily transported between country estate and town house.

Potted wild boar in Marsala wine and rosemary

Wild boar is a great favourite. Like all wild meats, it is very lean and dense and benefits from the extra fat that potting requires. Treat it like beef or pork: wild boar works either way.

Although it may seem like a good idea to buy the boar from the butcher ready diced, it is a safer bet to buy a piece that you cut up yourself. You can then be sure to cut away and discard any gristle or sinew before the meat goes into the marinade. Always avoid gristle as it spoils the mouth feel of the potted product.

The method is similar to that of confits. Cut the meat, avoiding sinew and gristle, into small pieces. Marinade and leave overnight or for 8 hours and drain. Add liquid and fat and then cook for 8 hours and pot.

One suggestion is to serve it on crostini with jelly (*see* Chapter 3).

Ingredients
- 350g shoulder of wild boar, venison, pork or beef

Marinade
- 3 small sprigs of rosemary
- 60ml Marsala wine
- 1 tablespoon of homemade plum ketchup (*see* page 89)
- ½ teaspoon sea salt
- ½ teaspoon ground black pepper
- 1 small shallot stuck with 4 cloves
- 2 cloves garlic

To cook
- 150g rendered pork fat
- 3 tablespoons of beef stock or miso
- Crumpled sheet of greaseproof or baking parchment
- Extra fat to seal

- 1 × 400g Kilner jar

Before you start
- Wash Kilner jars and jars with lids (if using) in hot soapy water, rinse, invert and put on a baking tray in a pre-heated oven at 125°C for 20 minutes to sterilize.
- The rubber gaskets, like lids, need boiling for 4 minutes, submerged in water.

1. Dice the meat and put in a shallow dish with the marinade ingredients.
2. Stir, cover with a cloth and leave for 8 hours or overnight.

Put the diced meat and marinade ingredients in a shallow dish.

Transfer the meat to a casserole dish.

When cooked, shred the meat using two forks.

Fill a jar and top up with the reserved juices.

Make sure that all the meat is below the surface.

Potted wild boar will keep in the fridge unopened for up to a month.

3 In the morning drain and reserve the marinade and transfer the meat to a casserole dish with a lid. Add the fat and 75ml of the marinade and the stock.

4 Crumple a sheet of baking parchment and run it under the cold tap, shake and use it to fill the space between the meat and the lid of the casserole. Put in the oven at 100°C and slow cook for 8 hours or overnight.

5 After this time the meat should be tender. Use two forks to shred the meat.

6 Pour off the juices and reserve.

7 Fill a 400g Kilner jar.

8 Pour the reserved juices over the shredded meat. Press the meat down gently with the back of a fork under the fat. Close the jar and tap gently on a folded tea towel to expel any air bubbles that may be trapped in the jar. Slide a skewer or fine knife blade down the side of the jar to release any remaining air pockets.

9 Leave to set hard in the fridge. When quite set, if all the juices, fat and stock have been used up and the meat is not completely covered, melt a little extra fat to top up the jar.

10 Seal the jar. It will keep like this for a month in the fridge, but be sure to use it up quickly once opened.

Potted diced shoulder of venison with red wine and redcurrant jelly

Serve the potted venison for light lunches and starters, in tiny pies, on a watercress salad with pomegranate wedges or on crostini topped with redcurrant jelly and with an aperitive.

Makes 1 × 500g jar or 4 × 125g jars as gifts

Ingredients

- 500g shoulder of venison or wild boar
- 200ml red wine
- 1 blade of mace
- 1 heaped teaspoon of juniper berries, crushed
- ½ stick cinnamon
- ½ teaspoon ground black pepper
- 1 teaspoon sugar
- 1 teaspoon salt
- 2 tablespoons redcurrant jelly
- 150g rendered pork fat
- A crumpled sheet of greaseproof or baking parchment
- Extra fat to seal

Use the method for the recipe above for potted wild boar in Marsala wine and rosemary, adding the redcurrant jelly at step 3 with the stock and the fat.

POTTED FISH

These potted fish recipes are not intended to be kept for long. The ramekins provide one-portion servings that can be frozen if you do not wish to use them straight away.

Potted shrimp

There is no finer way to enjoy these meaty little brown fellows than when they are encased in butter. It is one of those rare, yet simple pairings, made in heaven. For a variation you can use strips of lobster tails.

Serve as a starter with Melba toast. The quantities given serve four.

Ingredients

- 300g cooked peeled brown shrimps
- 225g salted butter
- Pinch ground white pepper, cayenne, ground mace and nutmeg

- 4 ramekins, washed in soapy water
- Pre-heat oven to 160°C/Gas Mark 3

Crostini

Crostini keep in an airtight tin for weeks, providing an instant base on which to serve the potted meat and fish, rillettes and rillons in these recipes. It is a good way to use up stale baguettes.

Serve topped with rillettes, rillons, confit and potted meat and fish. These quantities should make 30 crostini.

- 1 baguette, at least a day old
- Extra-virgin olive oil
- 2 or 3 cloves garlic cut in half cross-wise

Cut the baguette diagonally into 1cm-thick slices, arrange on a baking tray and drizzle with extra-virgin olive oil. Set in a pre-heated hot oven (200°C/Gas Mark 6/7) and cook until golden, say 10–15 minutes. Turn and cook for another 5–10 minutes on the other side. When ready take out of the oven, rub with garlic and leave to cool.

Potted shrimp serving suggestion.

Make the clarified butter.

Add the spices and shrimps, and stir well.

Pack the shrimps into ramekins and top with clarified butter.

Make sure the shrimps are covered in a thin layer of clarified butter.

Serve with Melba toast or thinly sliced brown toast.

1 Melt the butter in a small saucepan over low heat.
2 Take the pan off the heat and leave to stand for a few minutes.
3 Carefully pour off the clarified butter that has risen to the surface.
4 Discard the cloudy milk solids on the bottom.
5 Reserve a quarter of the clarified butter for later use. Return the remainder to the pan. Add the spices and shrimps, stir well and cook over low heat for 2 minutes.
6 Pack the cooled shrimps into ramekin dishes and top with the clarified butter. Transfer the ramekins to a shallow ovenproof dish, add boiling water so that it comes halfway up the ramekins and cook in the pre-heated oven for 15 minutes. Leave to cool.
7 Top up each ramekin with a thin layer of the remaining clarified butter, making sure that the shrimps are completely submerged. Put in the fridge to set.
8 Take the potted shrimps out of the fridge 30 minutes before required. Push a small palette knife down the side of the ramekin while the butter is still cold and hard. This should dislodge the cushion of butter and shrimp from the pot. If not, start to run the palette knife around the edge until it does. Turn the potted shrimps out with a good firm shake onto a serving plate. Leave to return to ambient temperature.
9 Serve garnished with a few leaves and Melba toast or thinly sliced brown toast.

Clarified butter

- Melt the butter in a small pan over low heat and leave to stand for 10 minutes.
- The milk solids will sink to the bottom under the clarified butter.
- The clarified butter will rise to the top.
- Pour this off and reserve.
- Discard the milk solids.
- Pour the clarified butter over the meat or fish to be potted, once it has been cooked in a bain-marie, and leave to set hard.

If preferred, spices and herbs can be added to the butter while it is being melted. Pour off the flavoured clarified butter and sieve if necessary.

Clarified butter is used both as an ingredient and as a seal for pastes and spreads, such as potted meats and fish, and for specialities such as potted shrimp and crab.

Potted Newlyn crab with chilli and thyme

Both white and brown crab meat should be enjoyed unadulterated to savour the full flavour and potting enables just that. This is a brilliant way to use brown crab meat and those pots of crab meat that are 90 per cent brown meat and 10 per cent white. Simply scrape off the white meat and set aside for garnish.

Serve with rocket and Melba toast or hot buttered brown toast. The quantities given serve four.

Ingredients

- 250g brown crab meat
- 150g salted butter
- A few sprigs of thyme leaves
- ½ teaspoon of chilli flakes
- Juice of 1 small lemon
- Salt and coarsely ground black pepper
- Extra sprigs of thyme for serving

- 4 buttered ramekins or 500ml ovenproof pot

Pre-heat the oven to 160°c/Gas Mark 2

Potted crab ingredients.

1 Put the butter in a small pan, add a few sprigs of thyme and the chilli flakes, and set over low heat to melt.
2 When the butter has melted, take the pan off the heat and leave it to stand for a few minutes. Then carefully pour off the clarified butter through a sieve to catch any bits of thyme or chilli that may have escaped.
3 Reserve the clarified butter.
4 Discard the cloudy milk solids, the thyme and chilli that is left in the pan.
5 Put the brown meat in a blender, add half the cooled butter, the juice of a lemon and salt and pepper and mix until smooth. Taste and add extra seasoning if necessary.

Melt the butter with a few sprigs of thyme and the chilli flakes.

Put the brown meat, half the cooled butter, the juice of a lemon and salt and pepper in a blender.

Transfer the smooth crab mixture to the pot or ramekins.

Place the pot or ramekins on an ovenproof dish and pour enough boiling water around them to go halfway up their sides.

Seal the crab meat with the reserved clarified butter and top with a sprig of thyme.

Serve potted Newlyn crab with crusty bread or Melba toast.

6 Put the crab mixture in a single pot or divide between the ramekins.

7 Level and smooth the mixture.

8 Transfer to a suitable ovenproof dish, add boiling water so that it comes halfway up the sides of the dish or dishes and cook for 25 minutes in the pre-heated oven.

9 Wipe away any splashes of potted crab from the side of the dish and leave to cool. Pour a film of the reserved clarified butter over the top to seal the crab meat and top with a sprig of thyme. Put in the fridge to set.

10 Take the potted crab out of the fridge 20 minutes before serving to bring back to ambient temperature. If using ramekins, run a palette knife around the edge of the ramekins and turn out, butter side down (*see* the potted shrimp recipe above).

11 If using a single dish, simply spoon out and serve with crusty bread or Melba toast.

Potted curried haddock

This winning pairing of smoked haddock and curry powder was inspired by the classic kedgeree combination. Use this recipe for salmon, adding the juice of a lemon and a level teaspoon of ground cumin. For mackerel, add two teaspoons of horseradish and omit the curry powder.

Ingredients

- 200g thick natural smoked haddock
- 150g butter clarified butter (*see* page 148)
- Salt and pepper to taste
- 1 level teaspoon curry power

1. Put the haddock in a pan and cover with cold water. Bring gently to simmering point and cook on low heat for 20 minutes or until it starts to flake. Strain and put on a plate.
2. Gently scrape the fish off the skin in flakes and remove and discard any bones using tweezers.
3. Put the clarified butter in a pan.
4. Return the flaked haddock to the pan, add the curry powder and mix carefully so as not to break the fish flakes. Simmer for 2 minutes.
5. Transfer the buttered haddock to a small bowl, level, top up with clarified butter. Refrigerate and leave to cool.
6. Serve at ambient temperature with crusty bread, toast or Melba toast.

This recipe also works with salmon, adding lemon and cumin.

Carefully remove any remaining bones with tweezers.

Return the flaked haddock to the pan with the clarified butter and carefully mix in the curry powder.

Serve with crusty bread, toast or Melba toast.

THE REMAINS OF THE DAY: SPREADS AND PASTES

Potting is a satisfying way of using up small quantities of leftovers, be they roast meats, game, cooked ham, casseroles, poached or smoked fish or the remains of your cheese board. As often happens, there is not enough left to make a meal but too much to waste. This is where pastes and spreads come in.

Children of the 1950s and 1960s were brought up on bread and butter or sandwiches spread with pastes made with crab, chicken, salmon or beef. These were not necessarily homemade, indeed they were probably made by Shippam's of Chichester, who have been developing savoury sandwich spreads since the eighteenth century, when potting was still a big thing.

Back then making pastes and spreads was quite a chore. There were no food processors and the meat and fish had to be laboriously pounded and sieved. This is convenience food at its best, so start making your own with those bits in the fridge you will probably end up throwing away.

Don't reserve them for the kids either. Spice them up and add a dash of sweet sherry, Marsala wine, port or brandy, along with cream, butter, leftover sauces and so on. Serve them to grown-ups on toast with drinks, as light lunches with salad, as starters with Melba toast or as a quick snack with crusty bread.

Pot in small ramekins, which can then be frozen, thawed and used as needed. Alternatively you could use small Kilner jars or bowls.

Potted ham

Ingredients

- 150g cooked ham
- 50g clarified butter (*see* page 148)
- 1 teaspoon Dijon mustard
- 1 tablespoon thick cream
- 50ml ham stock or parsley sauce
- 1 tablespoon of medium sweet sherry or Marsala wine
- Good pinch of mace or cumin
- Good pinch of cayenne or coriander
- 2 tablespoons finely chopped parsley
- Salt and pepper to taste
- 75g clarified butter to finish (*see* above)

Equipment

- 3 buttered ramekins or single ovenproof dish

Potted ham ingredients.

Pre-heat oven to 160°c/Gas Mark 3.

1   Put the meat in a blender with the stock, alcohol and the other ingredients (except the parsley). Reduce to a moist paste. Taste to make sure it is processed well: the finished spread should be smooth and creamy. Then add the chopped parsley and taste for salt and pepper.
2   Press the mixture into ramekins or an ovenproof dish.
3   Transfer to a roasting tray, add boiling water to come halfway up the sides of the dish or dishes and cook in the pre-heated oven for 20 minutes (30 minutes if using a single dish). Leave to cool.
4   Cover with the clarified butter (*see* page 148).
5   Leave to set in the fridge. Press a herb leaf or other distinguishing ingredient in the middle of the butter while it is still soft. Once the butter sets the contents of the pot is no longer visible.
6   Bring back to ambient temperature before serving with slices of hot toast or crostini, Melba toast or soda bread and chutney.

When potting, press the processed mixture into an ovenproof dish or ramekins, level, then cover with clarified butter.

Press a leaf or another distinguishing sign into the butter to help identify the contents.

Potted chicken or turkey with gherkins

Ingredients

- 150g cooked chicken or turkey
- 60ml cream or thick yoghurt
- 50m gravy or stock
- 1 heaped teaspoon of Dijon mustard
- Grinding of black pepper
- Good pinch of allspice
- A few drops of Tabasco
- Pinch of salt to taste
- 8 gherkins, finely chopped
- 75g clarified butter to pot (*see* page 148)

Prepare as above. Put all the ingredients except the gherkins and the butter in a food processor and blend until smooth, then stir in the finely chopped gherkins and taste for seasoning.

Press into the ramekins or a single pot and transfer to a roasting tin. Add enough boiling water to come halfway up the pots and set in a pre-heated oven at 160°c for 20 minutes, 30 minutes for a single pot.

Serve potted ham with slices of hot toast.

Potted wild boar with mushrooms

Ingredients

- 150g leftover roast boar, venison, beef or pork or other game meats
- 100ml gravy
- 1 good tablespoon mushroom ketchup (*see* Chapter 5)
- ¼ teaspoon ground mace or nutmeg
- ½ teaspoon ground cayenne pepper
- A grinding of black pepper
- 15ml lemon juice
- Salt to taste
- 75g clarified butter (*see* page 148)

Prepare as above. Put all the ingredients in a blender and work until smooth and taste for seasoning. Press into the ramekins or a single pot and transfer to a roasting tin. Add enough boiling water to come halfway up the pots and set in a pre-heated oven at 160°C for 20 minutes.

Potted salmon with capers

Ingredients

- 150g hot smoked or leftover poached salmon
- 1 lime
- 100g/ml mascarpone, crème fraiche or double cream
- Good pinch of salt
- Good pinch of cayenne pepper
- 1 tablespoon salted capers, rinsed, dried and chopped
- 75g clarified butter (*see* page 148)

Prepare as above. Put all the ingredients other than the capers in a food processor and blend until smooth. Stir in the finely chopped capers and taste for seasoning. Press into the ramekins or a single pot and transfer to a roasting tin. Add enough boiling water to come halfway up the pots and set in a pre-heated oven at 160°C for 20 minutes, or 30 minutes for a single pot.

Potted cheese

This recipe can be varied to suit your taste or what you have available. Experiment with your own combinations of cheeses and seasonings. It is a thrifty way to use up odd bits of leftover cheese. Add a good pinch of paprika, cayenne, mustard powder, nutmeg, mace and a few drops of Worcester or Harrison's sauce, anchovy essence or other seasoning.

Try adding port, wine or brandy for a luxurious finish. You have nothing to lose but your leftovers.

Ingredients

- 160g of cheese, grated or crumbled
- 60g salted butter, softened
- A slug of dry sherry, sauterne or Worcester or Henderson's sauce
- A pinch of nutmeg or mace, cayenne
- Salt and freshly ground black pepper
- A little clarified butter for sealing (*see* page 148)

In a food mixer, or in a bowl with a wooden spoon, beat together the cheese, softened butter, sherry and nutmeg until fairly smooth. Taste, add salt and pepper if necessary, then spoon into a bowl or jar, and pour over some clarified butter to seal.

Covered and refrigerated, this will keep for several weeks. Serve with oatmeal biscuits and a dab of chutney or fruit paste.

Potted Stitchelton

Stitchelton is a unique farm-made blue cheese produced on the Welbeck Estate in Nottinghamshire. It is one of the few cheeses still made with raw milk, which allows the cheese's flavour and texture to vary with the seasons and as it matures. This, weirdly, is the only reason that stops it being called Stilton, which according to its Protected Designation of Origin (PDO) is only made with pasteurized milk. For a list of stockists, contact Neal's Yard Dairy (www.nealsyarddairy.co.uk).

Ingredients

- 25g butter for sealing
- 150g Stitchelton or Colston Basset Stilton or a combination of 100g of blue cheese and 50g of cream cheese at room temperature
- 50g softened butter
- 25ml white port or other fortified or dessert wine or spirit, such as sherry, Marsala or cognac
- A few drops of Worcester sauce
- Salt and freshly ground black pepper

- 1 × 250g jar with lid or Kilner jar

1. First make the clarified butter. Put the butter for sealing in a small pan on low heat and leave until melted, then switch off the heat and transfer to a bowl and leave to stand while you work the cheese.
2. In a food mixer, or in a bowl with a wooden spoon, beat the Stitchelton and cream cheese together with the softened butter, alcohol and aromatics until smooth. Taste, add salt and pepper if necessary, then spoon into a bowl or jar.
3. Pour a thin layer of the clarified butter over the cheese to seal the jar, taking care to leave the solids at the bottom of the bowl. Seal the jar with a lid and refrigerate.

    This will keep for several weeks. Serve with your favourite cheese biscuits, Melba toast or crostini and grapes or celery.

Variations

Potted Caerphilly and apricot

- Finely grate 125g Caerphilly and proceed as above, omitting the alcohol and aromatics. Finely chop 25g dried apricots, stir in and beat again.

Goats cheese with dried tarragon and Sauternes

- Cream 150g soft goat's cheese with a teaspoon of finely chopped dried tarragon and 20ml Sauternes, then proceed as above, omitting the alcohol and aromatics, but adding Marsala wine.

Melba toast

Wafer-thin crisp and curled Melba toast is the perfect accompaniment to finely pounded potted cheese, meat and fish. It's a bit of a fiddle to make, but well worth the effort as it can be made in advance and stored in a tin until required.

8 slices of medium-sliced white bread
Preheat the grill to medium to high heat.

1. Toast the bread on both sides.
2. Cut the crusts off.
3. Using a serrated bread knife, carefully cut the toast horizontally through each slice of bread, pressing down with the flat of your left hand while cutting with the right or vice versa.
4. You will end up with 16 paper-thin slices of bread, toasted on one side and white on the other.
5. Set the grill to medium and return the toast to the grill pan, white side up. The thin toast will brown and curl up in the heat of the grill. Transfer to a wire rack and leave the Melba toast to cool.

Keep in a tin until required. Serve cold in a basket with butter.

The tricky bit – cutting the slice horizontally with a serrated bread knife.

Return the toast to the grill, white side up.

SOTTO OLIO – GOLDEN POTTING

Turning to Italy and the Mediterranean we find olive oil as the potting medium of choice. Meat and fish are simmered in stock flavoured with herbs, spices and garlic, cooled and then preserved in oil. Tuna is a popular choice, but we are going to use rabbit. Variations will be given for chicken and tuna.

Potted rabbit with extra-virgin olive oil, sage and garlic (tonno di coniglio)

This antipasto from Piedmont in Northern Italy is a popular rustic dish made when rabbit is plentiful. The meat is gently simmered in an aromatic vegetable broth, pulled to pieces and then potted in extra-virgin olive oil with sage and garlic.

Its Italian name, *tonno di coniglio*, literally means 'rabbit tuna'. The rabbit is preserved the way that tuna is prepared and packed in the neighbouring coastal region of Liguria. Piedmont is one of the few Italian regions to be landlocked, but has lush green hillsides and tracts of wild woodland where rabbits abound. Hence this delicious and unusual culinary tradition. Try making it with chicken or guinea fowl, if you are not keen on rabbit.

Put the rabbit or chicken in a pan, together with the ingredients as directed.

White scum will form on the surface, which should be skimmed off and discarded.

It is delicious eaten straight away, but it was made traditionally to preserve the tender, young white meat. It should be kept for a month before opening to appreciate its full flavour and will keep for six months.

It is good served on crostini with an aperitif, as part of a mixed antipasto platter, in a salad as a starter or light lunch dish such as Salad Niçoise, or indeed any way you would normally serve tinned tuna.

When using extra-virgin olive oil for potting, the finished product must be pasteurized (for full details of the process, *see* page 23.)

Ingredients

- 1 skinned rabbit, cut into pieces and washed thoroughly
- 1 onion
- 1 carrot
- 1 stick of celery
- 1 bay leaf
- A few stems of flat leaf parsley
- 3 cloves garlic, skinned
- A good sprig of sage or 6 large leaves
- Plenty of extra-virgin olive oil
- 1 heaped teaspoon salt crystals and extra for seasoning
- Freshly ground black pepper

- 1 × 500ml or 2 × 250ml preserving jars

Before you start

- Wash Kilner jars, or jars with lids, in hot soapy water, rinse, invert and put on a baking tray in a pre-heated oven at 125°C for 25 minutes to sterilize.
- The rubber gaskets, like lids, need boiling for 4 minutes, submerged in water. Drain on a clean cloth.

1 Put the onion, carrot, celery, herbs and coarse sea salt in a pan with the rabbit or chicken.
2 Cover with cold water and bring gently to the boil.
3 White scum that forms on the surface should be skimmed off and discarded.
4 Cover with a lid and simmer over low heat for 90 minutes.
5 After this time, switch off the heat and leave the ingredients in the water for an hour.

6 After an hour transfer the rabbit or chicken to a colander to drain. Transfer to the fridge overnight.

7 The following morning pull the meat off the bones, it will come away easily. Tear or cut the white/pink meat into equal-sized strips. Discard any discoloured meat. Season to taste with crushed salt crystals. Crush the peeled garlic with a knife and divide each clove into 3 or 4 pieces. Discard any green shoots from the middle.

8 Pack the strips of meat into the jar or jars almost to the top, adding herbs and a piece of garlic here and there. Press down gently with a fork.

9 Cover the meat with extra-virgin olive oil. Tap the jar gently on a folded cloth every now and then, to make sure there are no air pockets trapped between the pieces of meat. Add extra oil, if necessary, until the level settles and the meat is completely covered.

10 Seal the jar.

11 The jars must be pasteurized for keeping. For full details and illustrations, *see* page 23.

12 Label and store in the dark. Use after one month when the flavour has fully developed.

13 Bring back to room temperature before using.

Variations

You can make this with two chicken breasts or a whole chicken. I like to cook a whole chicken and then enjoy the bone broth. (Once the chicken is cooked, transfer to a colander to drain. Boil the broth to reduce by half, then season with salt and pepper to taste.) I use the breast meat for this recipe and the leg meat for a chicken salad.

Chicken tuna: chicken and thyme
- 1 small chicken
- 1 onion
- 1 carrot
- 1 stick of celery
- 2 sprigs of thyme
- 1 bay leaf
- A few stems of flat leaf parsley
- 3 cloves garlic, skinned
- Sprigs of thyme for potting
- Plenty of extra-virgin olive oil
- Coarse salt
- Use the above method

Drain the rabbit or chicken in a colander.

As you pack strips of meat into the jar, sprinkle in herbs and pieces of garlic.

When any air pockets have been removed and the meat is completely covered in olive oil, seal the jar.

Tonno sott'olio (tuna and fennel in extra-virgin olive oil)
- 400g best tuna
- 1 onion
- 1 carrot
- 1 stick of celery
- 70g fennel
- 2 bay leaves
- A few stems of flat leaf parsley
- 3 cloves garlic, skinned
- A teaspoon of chilli flakes
- Plenty of extra-virgin olive oil
- Coarse salt

Rinse the tuna thoroughly to ensure there is no blood coming out of it, cook as above for 1 hour, then leave to drain for 24 hours, covered in the fridge. Break it up loosely with a fork and immerse in oil with garlic and chilli flakes. Use the method described above and ensure the jars are pasteurized.

Index

......